C000263584

CHRIS TARRANT
THE BIOGRAPHY

CHRIS TARRANT
THE BIOGRAPHY

VIRGINIA
BLACKBURN

metro

Published by Metro Publishing Ltd,
3, Bramber Court, 2 Bramber Road,
London W14 9PB, England

First published in hardback in 2003

ISBN 1 84358 081 0

All rights reserved. No part of this publication may be reproduced,
stored in a retrieval system, or in any form or by any means, without
the prior permission in writing of the publisher, nor be otherwise
circulated in any form of binding or cover other than that in which it is
published and without a similar condition including this condition
being imposed on the subsequent publisher.

British Library Cataloguing-in-Publication Data:

A catalogue record for this book is available from the British Library.

Design by www.envydesign.co.uk

Printed in Great Britain by CPD (Wales)

1 3 5 7 9 10 8 6 4 2

© Text copyright Virginia Blackburn 2003

Papers used by Metro Publishing are natural, recyclable products made
from wood grown in sustainable forests. The manufacturing processes
conform to the environmental regulations of the country of origin.

The publishers are grateful to the *Daily Express* for supplying all the
pictures in this book.

Every attempt has been made to contact the relevant copyright-holders,
but some were unobtainable. We would be grateful if the appropriate
people could contact us.

www.blake.co.uk

CONTENTS

1	Man with a Mission	1
2	A Glimmer of Light	21
3	Anarchy Rools OK	35
4	It Really Was OTT	55
5	Now We Are Two	75
6	Tarrant Returns To TV	93
7	Chrissy-Wissy Wins Again	111
8	The Full Chrissy	129
9	Now Everyone's a Winner	149
10	A Right Royal Stitch-Up	169
11	A Sadder and Wiser Tarrant	189
12	The Trials and Tribulations of Tarrant	207
13	Who Wants to be a Millionaire?	227
14	The Man Who Wanted to be a Millionaire – Too Much	247

MAN WITH A MISSION

'Are you sure you want to go for that one?' asks Chris Tarrant, leaning forward and giving the terrified contestant a searching glance. 'Is that your final answer?' The contestant nods, much as a rabbit would do in the glare of the spotlight, Tarrant opens his mouth to tell him whether he's won and – 'We'll be back right after the break!' yells Chris. Both contestant and audience, in *Who Wants To Be A Millionaire?*, the most successful game show ever, visibly wilt. Tarrant, having yet again drawn the maximum tension out of an already fraught moment, sits back and smiles.

Tarrant is, without a doubt, at the absolute peak of his profession. And it has been an extraordinary rise for a man who was a loner as a child, who went on to university to read English Literature, and who contemplated a career in teaching. But his is a rise typical of post-war Britain, where a once great empire turned into Cool Britannia – and where show business stars became the aristocracy of the day.

Chris Tarrant was born just after the war on October 10, 1946 in Reading. His father, Basil, worked his way up from being the tea boy to managing director of a company that made biscuit tins, while his mother, Joan, was a housewife. 'I was an only child, raised in Reading, Berkshire,' he recalled. 'Dad worked for a firm called Huntley Boorne & Stevens – their claim to fame was that they made the tins for Huntley & Palmer to put their biscuits in. Reading always smelled of biscuits and Dad brought big bags of broken ones home as a treat, every Friday.'

The young Chris was a happy little boy and the centre of attention at home. He once spoke about an early memory: 'I was given a cowboy outfit when I was three,' he said. 'I managed to tear it and lose my cap gun by Boxing Day.' He was very close to his grandfather, whom he regarded as his best friend and who instilled in him a love of the countryside that lasts to this day.

Home life, fittingly, was rather eccentric. 'Dad was a major during the war and our house was full of German memorabilia,' Tarrant said. 'We had an old bomb shell in one corner, a swastika flag in another and pictures of Hitler dotted about the place. I used to wonder which side Dad was on until I realised they were things he'd captured during the war. He was a member of the Moths – the Memorable Order of Tin Hats – but he didn't tell war stories.'

Indeed, Tarrant senior was prone to sitting in silence, reading and recalling his war years, without talking about them to his son. But theirs was not a melancholic household; liveliness also ran in the family. One of the greatest assets in shaping his career has been Chris's congeniality, an ability instantly to empathise with listeners, viewers, contestants – whoever it is he is dealing with. Tarrant also has the ability to create an air of slight anarchy, something that was clearly inherited from older members of his family. 'My life has been awash with lunatics,' he wrote in his autobiography *Tarrant Off The Record*.

'My dear old granddad was mad as a March hare. My dad, to this day a very successful businessman, is still a few peas short of a casserole. I grew up assuming there were thousands of kids out there with dads called Basil. Only, of course, there weren't. No one in their right mind is called Basil. I've only ever heard of two others in my entire life – one is Basil Fawlty, the other Basil Brush.'

In fact, father and son are alike in that they can both be the life and soul of the party and then both go off into periods of silence for hours – in Chris's case, when he is fishing. His father, like Chris himself, was strict and yet not averse to having fun with his son. 'I had a huge respect for him from an early age,' Tarrant said in an interview in the mid-90s. 'If he promised anything, he'd stick to it. All part of a military training, I suppose. He was a very silly dad, although I mean that in a kind way. He'd play football in the

3

garden with me and the kids next door. He gave us a rollicking for kicking the ball towards the house, but it was he who broke the French windows pretending to be Bobby Charlton. He's just as ridiculous with his grandchildren. He loves climbing around with my three-year-old, yet he'll pretend it's my mother who's desperate to see her grandchildren.'

Chris's very first memory is of a time when he was still little more than a toddler. 'When I was a little chap, the nice lady who lived in the flat upstairs called Auntie Esme was keeping an eye on me while my parents went to the pictures,' he later recalled. 'I had woken up and was running around looking for my mum and dad because I'd forgotten they were going out. I wasn't even three but I have an absolutely clear memory of Auntie Esme saying, "Don't worry, they'll be back soon," giving me a cuddle and putting me back to sleep.'

When Chris was four, he started what was to become his greatest hobby. 'I wish I'd gone fishing at an even earlier age,' he claimed. 'I didn't start until four – all those wasted years.' In his love of fishing, Tarrant was simply following a family tradition. 'Fishing was then a religion for the men in our family,' he wrote in *Ready Steady Go!*, an account of growing up in the 1950s and 60s. 'Granddad had fished all his life and his granddad before him and my dad had me sitting beside (and occasionally in) the River Thames with my own little cane rod from the age of four.

'We fished the Thames at Sonning and the River Kennet at

Newbury ... Considering our lack of skill, we caught a lot of fish. Mostly they were returned to the river, although occasionally my dad would proudly push me home on my bicycle with a fat pike tied to the cross bar. The unfortunate pikes would inevitably end up chucked to the local cats. Sometimes, under pressure from Dad and I, Mum would try to cook one of these muddy creatures and invariably, for all my mother's cooking skills, they would taste like a boiled blanket. On those nights the local cats had to wait a little longer but eventually they had a rare cooked tea thrown over the fence instead of the usual raw one.'

And something else happened too. At the age of four, Chris started primary school, which he did not enjoy. He remembers the teachers dressing in dull, dark colours and getting very carried away with using the cane. The 1950s were a dreary time in which to be growing up: post-war rationing was still in operation, the country was finding its feet again – and realising it had lost some of its standing in the wider world, despite winning the war – and life seemed less than exciting. With the onset of the 1960s, which coincided with Tarrant becoming a teenager, all that was to change – but life as a small-town boy lacked lustre. As he grew older he started bunking off school to take part in his two favourite activities: fishing and trainspotting.

Life was an innocent affair: Tarrant later recalled his delight when, aged six, he learned to swim, and his grief when his hamster Goldie died. 'We buried him in the back garden and put up a little cross,' he said.

The family was close knit and would take holidays together in the country. 'Early holidays with my parents and grandparents were always in Cornwall and it was always bloody raining,' he recalled. 'But I loved the traditional seaside activities like fishing in rock pools. Being an only child wasn't a problem because there was usually some other little boy to chum up with. We travelled to Cornwall by train until the momentous year when Granddad bought a car. This was the 1950s, when the AA man would salute an AA member. Even with hardly any other cars on the road it took hours to get there.

'One year, when I was about eight, we stayed on a farm in Cornwall. I helped with the milking, rounded up cows, played with the farm dogs. That was an idyllic holiday for me. I'm quite a little country bumpkin, really. Growing up in Berkshire, I was always into bird nesting and fishing.'

Like many only children, Chris spent his earliest years playing by himself. 'I played all the parts,' he explained. 'I always captained England and we won by one goal and I was always centre-forward. People say, "Didn't you miss having brothers and sisters?" but you just don't because you haven't got any. I find now that I've got a big family of my own it's really weird; all the fighting, the cuddling up at night, all that stuff. I never had that.'

Chris's first great friend was called Geoff Davy, whom he met at primary school. 'Geoff was a really nice kid from Bristol,' Tarrant said. 'I was better than him at fishing, at football, and my bike was faster than his. I had quite sticky-out ears in those days but Geoff's were huge – real car door jobs. So that was good too.'

Like many little boys, Chris became a boy scout, where he acquired the unlikely nickname Cuthbert, because it was the sort of name given to accident-prone and clumsy boys who could be a bit idiotic. It seems he deserved it. His mother Joan remembered one occasion when the young Chris got into a scrape with the scouts: the scout master called saying, 'I'm afraid I have bad news of Cuthbert.' The young Tarrant had crawled up on to a garden roof while trying to retrieve another cub's cap that had fallen from a tree, and fell through the garage roof. 'Wait till your father gets home,' warned Joan.

That meant that Chris was in real trouble. Basil loved his son, but he was a disciplinarian and one who kept the young Tarrant towing the line. 'Dad was very strict when I was younger and didn't relax with me until I turned 16,' Tarrant recalled. 'When Mum said she was going to smack me, she would warn me at least five more times before she actually hit me. If it was a "Wait till your father gets home" situation, I knew I was in serious trouble, although Dad only ever smacked me three times.'

On another occasion, he got into a rather worse scrape. 'I nearly drowned when I was about 11,' said Chris. 'I'd gone to Axmouth in Devon where the River Axe comes blasting out into the sea and sweeps everything before it, including silly little scouts learning to float on their backs. When I looked up, the beach was miles away. I hung on to a rock and was cut right across my chest and covered in blood when a fishing boat came to pick us up.'

Despite all his scrapes and silliness, Chris was a quiet little boy and nothing like the motor mouth he was to become. 'He was very easy-going and did as he was told,' Joan recalled. 'He would ask for things but, if we said no, he would accept it. He was quite a shy boy, although he did talk to people. He loved reading and fishing. I thought he might become a writer.'

When Tarrant talks now about his early childhood, he certainly makes it sound like the typical 1950s set-up – which, indeed, it was. He remains extremely proud of his father and his achievements. 'He was reasonably educated at state schools, he worked very hard and was the first person to get on-board outside the Huntley & Palmer family. He was also my best friend. Mummy was lovely. She loves her grandchildren to death and still hopes I'll get a proper job some day. Dad was very strict. It was "Wait till your dad gets home" and "What Dad says goes." He was very strict about bedtime. It was 8pm on the dot.

'They wanted me to achieve, get on, do my homework. But that's what everyone did then. You got on with it. I had to earn my pocket money and I learned the value of money. My dad was not an open chequebook, if I wanted something I had to earn half the amount. I'm the same with my kids now. They've got to learn to strive. I always worked hard, I had short-term ambitions. I just liked doing well, in exams and at sports.'

At 13 Tarrant was sent away to boarding school, King's School, Worcester. He hated it with a vengeance. 'I don't approve of single-sex boarding schools,' he once said. 'They are very unhealthy. I've been a ladies' man all my life.'

Nor did he like the day-to-day side of public-school life, especially fagging, the system that meant younger boys did chores for the older ones. 'I didn't like fagging,' he complained (with some justification). 'Why should I iron this git's trousers? I've never mastered ironing and I burned the trousers and then got caned.'

His parents, however, thought they were doing the best for their much cherished son. Although they were not badly off, neither were they extremely wealthy and sending Chris to school involved some financial sacrifice on their part. 'I think Mum and Dad had a very strong ethic,' he said, 'looking back on it – if you had any money to spare at all, you spent it on your child's education. Certainly, in the middle years, I think it must have been quite hard for Dad to pay the bills. We didn't have any holidays in those four years.'

And, despite his dislike of the place, Tarrant's personality began to develop. Gone was the quiet little boy who liked reading and in his place emerged a much tougher and more rebellious character, who was not always prepared to play by the rules. 'I remember a housemaster saying, "We have lots of boys go through the school, but not many are personalities,"' said Joan Tarrant. 'Chris was definitely a personality. He stuck out from the crowd.'

Basil Tarrant also remembered that his son turned out to

be rather more of a handful than he had been as a young child. 'He had paid education from the age of four, but it wasn't until he went to boarding school at 13 that it became apparent that he was a bit of a card,' he recalled. 'He'd only been there a year when the housemaster sent for me because Chris was the subject of a complaint by the German teacher. This teacher spoke with an accent that sounded like someone pretending to be foreign and Chris would mimic him, to the great amusement of the rest of the class.'

He clearly was something of a personality, but personalities do not necessarily fit in well with a very structured society. As he grew older, Chris's dislike of the school developed further, not least as he became increasingly rebellious – as, indeed, did his entire generation. 'I'm really sorry I can't make the right noises for King's School, but I wasn't happy there,' he said years after leaving. 'It was very much a boys-only minor public school and I didn't like the way you were all supposed to turn into little Hooray Henries. I was constantly in trouble.

'We were all young and rebellious. It was the 60s and we were all trying to grow our hair long, listening to Stones records, things like that. The public school system was one of the first things that came under attack by adolescents of that generation.'

And one occasion Chris considered faking a fall into the River Severn in order to escape punishment. In the book *Celebrity School Days*, compiled to raise money for Children In Need, he recalled yet another occasion on which he was late back to school. 'Some of the lengths I went to to get myself a good hiding were quite remarkable,' he recalled, 'like the night I was two and a half hours late back into school for evening call. Who's going to fuss about two and a half hours when a little lad's just been snatched from the jaws of eternity?'

Tarrant thus shinnied up a drainpipe, filled a bath, climbed in fully clothed and then marched to a prefect's study, where he claimed that he had fallen into the river while trying to rescue a cat. 'When I presented myself whimpering apologetically, all was forgiven,' he wrote. 'They sat me down in the big armchair usually reserved for the head boy and fussed all around me. Matron came rushing down, hot Bovril was provided and I sat there heroically telling how I'd been trying to save a little kitten from a tree when the branch had cracked, hurling me into the water.

'There was no question of being punished. They were just glad to have got me back safe and sound. At least they would have been if the duty prefect doing his rounds hadn't missed my dramatic arrival and come in asking, in all innocence, why there was a trail of wet footprints leading down two flights of stairs from one of the two bathrooms.'

It must be said that others remember Chris's school days differently. Tim Hickson, a master at the school when Tarrant was a pupil, said in an interview in 2003, 'I knew young Tarrant when he was here, although I never taught him. I would see him quite often coming out of one door. He was always larking about. A bright lad who seemed full of fun. He certainly never gave the impression he was desperately unhappy.

'As for being caned in front of the whole school, that was utter rubbish. I switched the television on the other night and he was on the Parkinson show. The two of them were goading each other about their school days, almost trying to prove who had the worse time. I just turned it off.' Whatever the exact truth, though, Tarrant clearly had no affection for his *alma mater*, once describing it as like 'a modern day Iran'.

But he had mates. His best friend was 'a tall, gangly boy called Mike Hulbert. We were sports mad and used to play a lot of silly records.' The pair also idolised the heroes of the time, especially Elvis Presley and Bobby Charlton. The times certainly were a-changing: Tarrant and his friends had all swapped their old-fashioned gramophone players, which needed to be wound up and played with a whole tin full of needles, for the Dansette Major, which did not have to be wound up and which needed only one needle. It was the beginning of a series of changes that would make music constantly available to everyone.

He also had the odd girlfriend, but the relationships were all extremely innocent. When Tarrant was 15 he had his first proper girlfriend – although it didn't last long. 'Babs Honeywell was a very pretty girl at the local grammar school and we were at the posh, spotty boarding school in Worcester,' said Tarrant. 'I was 15 and I'd been going out with her for two weeks when she wanted to call it off because

I was a bit of rough. I thought I was all right but she thought I was a bit self-centred and not very romantic, which I have to say is probably absolutely bang on.'

Tarrant consoled himself in time-honoured fashion: he took to drink. Asked when he had his first hangover, he confessed, 'It was probably the morning after Babs Honeywell dumped me. I used to have lots of very bad cider hangovers then. I saw this documentary once about the making of scrumpy and they'd throw a sheep into the vat and the cider would just dissolve it.'

Many years later the two were reunited on the television programme *Stars In Their Lives*. When Babs sauntered out on to the set, Tarrant at first didn't recognise her – until a picture flashed up of the 15-year-old Babs wearing a bikini. The penny dropped. 'I do remember you,' said a stunned Chris. 'You were a real raver.'

The real reason for the end of their romance came out when Babs rather ungallantly told the show that Chris was a lousy kisser. 'He would walk me to the top of the road and then slurp all over me,' she revealed. Tarrant took it in good part. 'I hadn't mastered tongues,' he said. 'I'm afraid I did have an unpleasant slurping technique. She opened her mouth and I nearly fell in.'

Tarrant could prove aggravating at home as well as at school. By the early 1960s youth culture was slowly taking off and it became fashionable for young men to wear their hair long. Chris promptly grew his hair, much to the disgust of his father. 'Hair was our biggest flash point because he didn't like me having it long when I was in my teens,' Tarrant recalled.

'I used to love swimming, so Mum came out with this cunning ruse that I would swim faster if I had short hair. Dad favoured a more direct approach and would shout at me to get it cut. This double onslaught eventually wore me down, so one day I did it myself and came downstairs looking like a monk. I don't think Dad was very impressed.'

Despite working hard, Tarrant claimed that he was not overly academic at school. 'I had no idea what I wanted to do,' he said. 'I was always good at sport and until about 15 or 16 I wanted to be captain of the English football team. Academically, I just seemed to get by.' He was being overly modest. In actual fact, Chris was showing quite a talent for English Literature, spurred on by a teacher.

There was, however, one major upset, when he failed one set of exams. Tarrant senior stepped in. 'We never had any serious arguments and only had one real man-to-son confrontation after I failed my mock O levels,' Tarrant junior recalled. 'He said, "What are you doing? Don't tell me all these teachers are mad." I told him not to worry and then worked hard and passed. I was afraid of disappointing him, not out of fear that he would hit the roof, it just seemed the worst thing in the world to let your father down.' The talk clearly worked: Tarrant gained nine O levels and four A levels.

He was also helped enormously by one teacher. 'Bobby Cash was my English teacher,' he said. 'He taught me that literature could be rewarding and fascinating. I remember reading a lot of Shakespearian comedies and thinking: this is obviously very funny and I'm very stupid because I don't find this remotely amusing. Bobby Cash got it all into perspective – he took things off the page and made it exciting. He encouraged me to read English at university.'

Chris took Cash's advice and went off to Birmingham University in 1964 to read English. He was much happier than he had been at school, although he was later to admit that the 'Swinging 60s' was something that was very much happening for other people. No matter. 'University was when I discovered girls and beer,' he said. 'You were very repressed at boarding school, so it became a bigger issue than ever.' It was also to provide Tarrant with his first opportunity to appear in front of an audience, when he appeared in a number of Shakespeare's plays.

But the 60s never really swung. Asked if the 60s had started when he was at university, he replied, 'No, had they hell! In Birmingham? I don't think I swung. I suppose we all thought we looked the bollocks in our flared trousers. I dunno. I just got the impression that David Bailey and Lord Lichfield were having every girl in England and no one else was getting a sniff. The revolution was that girls went on the pill and that did change a huge amount of their attitude towards their sexuality – and a damned good thing too.'

However, like many young men, Chris did have his fair share of tussles. Not usually an overly aggressive man, there was some aggro to be let out at university – possibly a reaction to all those canings – and it got out. 'I used to fight a lot when I was about 19,' he admitted later. 'It sounds a bit disturbing now but we used to roam around in gangs looking for a scrap. We'd have had a few beers, be hyped up and looking for trouble. It's sad and pathetic, but it's quite predictable among young men. It stopped when I grew up and also when I realised I could easily have a knife pulled on me.'

Money was often in short supply, which meant he had to resort to bizarre ways of trying to come by it – often involving his favourite hobby. 'In the *Angling Times* magazine, they used to run a competition called Find The Float,' he said. 'It was like "spot the ball" but you had to guess where the fishing float was. The prize was £300. I remember thinking, if I won that, I would never have to work again.'

But work he did. He took on a succession of jobs to supplement his grant, including one stint that he absolutely hated in a factory. Asked about his worst ever job, he replied, 'That's easy. Working on a conveyor belt, stacking books at a publishers when I was a student. It was a nightmare. I lasted a month, quietly going mad.' And it wasn't that well paid – Tarrant earned £3 7s 6d.

He also put money on the horses. 'I was really into horse racing,' he said. 'I used to study form every day. I took half my grant and put it on the horses each term. Usually I'd do really well. A couple of terms I was living on four times the grant. I used to spend it all on drink, of course. I drank Newcastle Brown Ale. We used to call it Journey Into Space. The benchmark was to go out and drink 20 pints.'

Chris's friends tended to be medical students rather

than fellow undergraduates studying English – and medical students have always had a reputation for wild living. These ones were no different. 'They were lunatics,' said Chris. 'They had this neat, surgical alcohol, which we used to mix with orange juice. It was rocket fuel. It was insane. But everything then was geared towards getting drunk. Once I woke up on a railway line just outside Wolverhampton lying between the sleepers. It scares me even thinking about it now.

'Because I came from a boys' school, it was the first time I'd mixed with girls in a big way. I lived on cheese and onion rolls, beer and 50p curries. The ladies must've had a great night out. I was trying to break the 20-pint barrier, my breath stank of onions and, if they were lucky, there'd be a curry on the way home.'

Nonetheless, somewhere along the line, Chris achieved that other great student goal: the loss of his virginity. It was not a memorable occasion. 'I was about 21 or 22 and it was in a Mini parked somewhere in Birmingham,' he confessed. 'I'd had far too much to drink. It was so, so very embarrassing – I couldn't even remember the girl's name afterwards. In fact, I really couldn't remember much of anything.' But, his goal accomplished, Chris was now ready to enter the world of real relationships.

He was also becoming increasingly passionate about fishing. Throughout his entire life, Tarrant has always been the keenest of keen anglers and it's not difficult to understand the appeal. Chris, after all, has to be incredibly outgoing in his professional life, so much so that it could almost become energy sapping if he had no other outlet for calm. Angling provides that outlet and it was a hobby he pursued as vigorously at university as he has done since.

Chris began to go abroad for the first time, spending summers with his friends. The holidays were cheap and cheerful affairs, as Tarrant himself freely admitted. 'After leaving school, I started going away with my mates, to quite horrible places on the Costa Brava,' he said cheerfully. 'Typical lads' holidays. About four of us, including my mate Ian "the Mod" from Stevenage, would pile into a beat-up Mini and blast it down to Spain at what felt like ridiculous speeds, but was probably only 60mph. We stayed in awful cheap hotels and primitive campsites. The entire time was spent fruitlessly chasing girls. Our diet consisted of paella, chips, Cognac and thin Spanish steaks that were never remotely beefy.'

Like many students, Chris affected a devil-may-care attitude, claiming that work came last on the agenda. Nonetheless, he managed to get a good degree. 'During university I did absolutely nothing for three years and got a 2:1,' he said. 'I read a lot, but it wasn't all on the curriculum. I certainly wouldn't have been sitting down and reading Jane Austen until midnight, although I did get into Yeats.' It is an ironic attitude – to make light of studying, given that the show he was to become most famous for was one that required a certain degree of academic knowledge. But then, Chris has always been a lot cleverer than he made out – after all, you don't end up with £20 million in the bank without some effort. Like so many people in Britain, Tarrant wanted to be a millionaire – and he did it, all of his own accord.

2

A GLIMMER OF LIGHT

When Tarrant graduated in 1967 he had no clear idea about what he wanted to do and drifted for a few years. 'I never really had a plan,' he said. In fact, Tarrant is in some ways the exception to the rule when it comes to a showbusiness career. Most people involved in radio or television have a blinding determination to get on: Chris simply didn't. 'I really drifted after university,' he said.

'I had no particular ambitions and, in a strange way, I still don't. There is simply an energy now and a momentum that takes over, but in those days I had no career thoughts at all.' Indeed, his first job was a very long cry from what was to become his career: 'I was a night security guard, then I drove lorries,' he later recalled. 'I was six-foot two and a bit of a gorilla. I used to load up lorries every morning with huge lawnmowers and drive to Manchester and Liverpool. I was Mr Yorkie Man. I was very happy.'

His father remembers the period well and has nothing but praise for his son's industry as he tried to work out what he really wanted to do. 'We never discussed his career while he was at university in Birmingham because I didn't see the point until he had his degree,' Basil recalled. 'By that stage he'd discovered women, so anything could have happened. He got a good second-class degree in English Literature, but couldn't get a job for the first six months after graduating, although he didn't lounge around. He never asked me for a penny and did various jobs to make money.'

It was an aimless time and one that continued, at the moment at least, to be so. He also worked as a bed salesman until, without really thinking about it, Chris drifted into teaching, where he earned the princely sum of £3,000 a year. This move was what ultimately brought him to a television career, through sheer chance and the people he met, but at the time he had no idea what lay ahead. He was simply living for the moment and so ended up at Samuel Pepys School in a rough area of south London.

'I just drifted into a teaching job,' Tarrant said many years later. 'I was living in London after university, short of cash, and one or two of my mates were teachers, and they said, "You can always get a job as a supply teacher if you've got a degree." Supply teaching basically means they send you to the worst schools in the whole of the inner London education area and they dutifully sent me off to this boys' school in New Cross;

they just said, "This is your class, Mr Tarrant, in you go ..." like throwing a pork chop to a hungry Rottweiler.'

Tarrant did not enjoy the experience. Coming from public school and university, it was a major culture shock to be thrown into an inner-city school and he experienced problems that were going to become even more prevalent in the English education system as the years wore on. 'I had 42 kids in my class,' he said. 'The initial problem was that a large percentage of this large, heaving class were not English-speaking – I mean, virtually no English at all. There were a lot of very, very large black kids, and even larger white kids, all with their Doc Marten boots up on the desk.

'Basically, they wanted it very much on their terms and, if you told them to sit down or shut up, immediately there was a problem. I come from a fairly cloistered academic background, and the idea of this sprawling mass of kids, doing what they liked, eating sandwiches, shouting and bawling at each other, effing and blinding, drawing obscenities on the blackboard, was totally opposite to anything I had ever seen. It was a shame, there were some very bright kids among them who hadn't a prayer of coming through the whole thing.'

And bear in mind, this was the end of the 1960s – well before the enormous inner-city school problems we know about today came to light. Tarrant did try, though, realising that the first and biggest problem he had to deal with was lack of discipline. 'You spent 95 per cent of the lesson just trying to get them to shut up,' he said. 'Luckily, because I'm six-foot two and was a lot bigger than most of the staff, I could actually get them to sit down and take out a book – although usually by the time you got as far as that, the bell went and they all went running off to set fire to somebody else's classroom.

'I couldn't believe the state of illiteracy; I found that a real shock. I remember after a couple of terms I just got so fed up with trying to wander through homework that had no beginning, middle or end, I actually did a lesson on the full-stop. That was for 15-year-olds! At first, I thought it an insult even to their intelligence but, for one of the few times in my teaching career, the class was absolutely spellbound: they were going, "Oh I see, so you put that little round thing there ..." Nobody had ever told them before.'

Tarrant was making a heroic effort but he was trying to resolve a problem for which there was no resolution. Inner-city schools are even worse now than they were then but, to his great credit, Chris really did struggle to help his pupils. But it didn't work. 'The full-stop was the peak, quite honestly,' he said with some degree of regret. 'From then on it was all downhill. I got very involved with one or two of the kids. You could see their little brains were actually thinking in very good images, and in a more sensible environment they could have done reasonably well, but it was bloody hard work.

'The moment they did do well, they'd get bullied; the whole ethos was one of not doing well and not succeeding in school, which was very much backed up by the parents. It was very noticeable that you would never get anywhere with the "Wait till I tell your father" sort of thing – there was every chance their father would come steaming across the playground and chin the teacher if he thought you were picking on his little Kevin.'

Difficult as matters were, however, Tarrant was learning a great deal about how tough life could be – and he did see some teachers who were battling against the odds. 'There were some amazing teachers there,' he said. 'Richard Cleall was the head and his relationship with the kids was fantastic. He would walk into a room of 15-year-old yobbos, hanging around looking menacing, and tell them to stand up straight. They'd say, "Sorry, sir" and do just as he said. It wasn't about frightening them – he commanded respect.'

Chris knew all along, however, that teaching was not ultimately what he wanted to do – and in latter years he spoke with some regret of the casual manner in which he treated his very short-lived career in the classroom. 'I'm not particularly proud of the way I drifted in and out of teaching,' he said. 'Some people see teaching as a soft option, but you shouldn't, because it shapes young lives. Teachers have to care. Those who have a vocation and a talent should be in the classroom – if you don't, you should go nowhere near it. It's too much responsibility.

'I was popular with students. I was just out of university and I think they saw me as a slightly older brother. I slept outside the school in a Mini van for six months; they thought that was great fun. I doubt if I was an inspiration to any of them. They are probably amused about the way I've turned out. I mean, it must be weird for them to see me on television and say, "He used to teach us."'

Perhaps they would not be surprised. For even now, watching *Who Wants To Be A Millionaire?*, it is still possible to see something of the teacher in Tarrant. That very slightly severe manner, that prompting and cross-questioning of the contestants – it is not impossible to imagine Chris in the classroom.

By the beginning of the 1970s, Tarrant was becoming increasingly downcast. He had been teaching for a year now and, while he still didn't know what he wanted to do, what he did know was that it was not to continue at the school. 'I spent an awful lot of time very depressed,' he said. 'I'd think, why am I doing this, and wonder what was the point of my learning Shakespeare and Jacobean tragedy – where was all this education going to lead me? It certainly wasn't doing me any good whatsoever there. I suppose I was still thinking, well, maybe one day there will be this vacancy in a nice little school in Dorset, it will be on the banks of a river and I'll be able to go fishing in between break times, and the kids will all be very bright and life will be wonderful.'

Thankfully for the man himself, it was not to be. But this was rapidly turning into one of the worst periods of Tarrant's life. Not only was he miserable in his professional life, but his personal life was equally unsatisfactory. It was a very unhappy time – and it was also the reason he ended up living in that van.

'This time also coincided with a desperate period in my

social life,' he later recalled. 'Probably because I was thoroughly fed up with the whole lifestyle I was leading, I had a monumental row with a then girlfriend, and did the classic thing of roaring off into the night: "That's it, I'm off …" I got about five miles down the road by one o'clock in the morning and suddenly thought, where do I live now?

'But I was resolved, whatever happened, that I would not go back and I lived in the Mini van, which I parked outside the school. It was bloody cold and February and March were pretty grim. One morning there was a knock on the windscreen and the postman said, "Mr Tarrant? 161 GLO?", which was the registration number of the van – I thought that was a great triumph, having my mail delivered there. But truthfully, living inside a Mini van was not a whole lot of fun.'

He swapped the van for another car, which made matters even worse in some ways – although at least he was not actually living in it. But he did keep attracting the attention of the police. 'After I sold the Mini van I got a yellow and black Mini Cooper S with very fat wheels and a huge exhaust pipe that used to make a ridiculous noise like a bee as I drove around London,' he said. 'I had shoulder-length blond hair and must have looked like a right villain because I used to get stopped several times a day by the police. In the end, I got used to it.'

But, as so often happens in life, just as Chris became convinced his life would never get better, quite suddenly it did. And ironically, it was through his teaching stint that Chris first got an inkling of what he would really like to do. Chris's career in entertainment really came about almost by chance, as he admitted later on. 'The husband of one of the teachers became a drinking mate,' he said. 'He was working at the Central Office of Information and told me they were setting up an overseas film unit. It was very civil service and planned to make films promoting Britain around the world. It had the advantage of an enormous budget and no real brief.'

This friend decided that Chris might just be the right person to work in this new and developing area and so suggested he come on board. 'He said to me after ten months at this school, "Do you want to come and work in television?"' Chris remembered. 'I asked him what use I would be with my knowledge of Jacobean tragedy.' (Tarrant had clearly read something, even if not Jane Austen.)

'He said, "Doesn't matter, come and be a researcher, that's a real bluffer's gig," and I left like a shot. I gave in the minimum notice – whatever it was, a week, a fortnight – and I was the hell out of it. I still think of my time there, even though it was a very long time ago. Some of the bigger kids still appear in my dreams, invariably villains; it's probably very unfair but some of them, I'm sure, because of their social backgrounds will have got themselves in all sorts of trouble.'

And so just like that, with a leap, he was free. Chris applied for a job and ended up working for the Central Office of Information, where he was to learn his trade. 'My mate suggested I join as a researcher and he'd teach me the ropes,' he said. 'In the next three years I learned everything about film making – writing, directing, cutting and editing.' He made a number of films, including one about a length of rope, a 12-second epic that won a prize in Romania.

Basil Tarrant was supportive. 'When he told me he was leaving [teaching] to go to the Central Office of Information, I wished him the best of luck,' he said, 'because I knew that if he couldn't take a chance when he was only 24, then he never would.'

His world had begun to expand in other ways, as well. Tarrant began to travel in his work, and when he was still young began a lifelong love affair with the Caribbean that continues to this day. 'The first time I went to the Caribbean, I was about 21 [sic],' he said later. 'I was doing some directing for the Central Office of Information and was sent to Trinidad. It was complete hell. Port of Spain was really aggressive and the tension was made worse because I was working with an all-black crew from New York.

'Since then I've been pretty much all over the Caribbean. It's one of my favourite escape places – it's predictably warm, the food is excellent and the people are incredibly friendly. When I was younger I didn't bother so much about winter breaks but now I'm doing *Millionaire* and Capital Radio, I'm usually desperate to get away by January. My favourite islands must be Grenada and St Lucia – they're great as long as you don't want anything done.

'In St Lucia I had arranged a trip into the jungle, but the woman wouldn't let me go until I promised not to eat any green parrots! The parrot is the emblem of the island and apparently some of the local kids had been stealing them for food. I don't like Barbados because it's full of English posers. My Caribbean golden rule is never to go anywhere where Michael Winner might come walking towards me dressed only in a thong.'

It was a strange time. 'The place was run by civil servants who hadn't a clue what they were in charge of,' he said. 'And the budget seemed infinite. I once spent four months in Trinidad, following a taxi driver from Brixton who had gone over there to learn more about the black way of life.'

On top of that, while he was working at the COI, Tarrant met Sheila, the woman who was to become his first wife. It was his first successful relationship (in as much as a relationship that ended in divorce could be successful): the two started dating and, this time, it was serious. Until Sheila, nothing had really worked, with Chris himself admitting to selfishness. 'I had always done exactly as I wanted to and couldn't understand if my girlfriend didn't want to do the same,' he later admitted. 'I'd say, "What do you mean you don't want to come fishing all night in the rain?"' It was, in fact, classic only-child behaviour. Children learn to negotiate through arguing with their siblings, something that Chris was not to learn until he was much older.

And now, having learned his trade at the COI, Tarrant decided it was time to move on. 'At 26 I decided to become a TV reporter,' he said. 'I'd seen these guys outside Buckingham Palace saying a few words and I thought, that looks a doddle.'

Having finally decided what he wanted to do with his life, Tarrant set out to make up for lost time. He leaped towards his new goal with gusto. 'I wrote to every TV company in Britain,' he said. 'The letter was ridiculous. One phrase went, "I am the face of the 70s. This is your last chance to snap me up." When I think about it now, I cringe.

'Most TV companies thought I was a prat. But Yorkshire TV and ATV in Birmingham both offered me a job. I chose ATV and started, on weekly contracts, on a magazine show as a reporter and newsreader. I never worry about short contracts, nor about getting the sack. I always feel: "Oh sod it, if they do get rid of me I'll go fishing, then think of something else to do." I stayed there four years. I was not very good at the straight stuff, I could read the news seriously but, when I did interviews, I could be unpredictable. My bosses started giving me the lighter items – the upside-down beer drinker or the man who slept up a tree. I enjoyed that. I found really nutty, quirky people absolutely fascinating.'

It was a talent he put to good use, taking on a sort of action man role for ATV Today, before going on to narrate the respected schools' programme *Stop, Look, Listen*. This lack of reverence was also to prove the making of him, for it not only provided Tarrant with his own screen persona, it also proved perfect for the programmes that he was later to front – and it quickly showed him that he didn't want to be a newsreader. 'You used to have to interview people and say, "With respect," when really what you wanted to say was, "You're a liar and I hate you."' He particularly loathed politicians and, of all politicians, he particularly loathed mayors. 'You wanted to punch them on the nose and say, "You're a lying bastard and

31

you're filling your bloody boots,"' he said. 'I wasn't very cool. I couldn't be Jeremy Paxman.'

He could, however, be a sex symbol. Chris and Sheila were by now involved in a serious relationship, but there are women for whom fame is an aphrodisiac and these women started showing an interest in Tarrant. He wasn't mega-famous, he wasn't a household name, but no matter. He was regularly appearing on television. And as he began to appear more often, so they began to find him increasingly attractive, approaching him whenever they got the chance. It was heady stuff for a young man not used to the limelight.

Asked if his attractiveness to women increased once he was on television, Chris replied, 'Yes – several girls in the same year found me attractive. They'd come up to me in pubs and take me off and interfere with me. It was great. All that just for reading the news in my Harry Fenton suits!'

It seemed harmless, but it was to turn into a problem. Although he was always perfectly attractive, Chris had never been Casanova and, after a repressed boarding-school existence, followed by a few miserable years finding his feet, becoming the centre of female attention was exhilarating. It was to run out of control, as Tarrant himself later confessed. But at the time he was simply enjoying himself in his new career, getting used to the limelight and preparing himself for what lay ahead.

And Chris's parents, Joan and Basil, were astonished at this turn in their son's fortunes, but also pleased and proud. The couple couldn't pick up ATV in Reading and so used to drive over to Oxford to watch their boy on Joan's sister's television. 'I never once doubted his talent,' his proud father said, greatly relieved that Chris had, at long last, found his chosen career. As for Chris himself, the 1970s and his work for ATV was about to make him famous beyond his wildest dreams – and all because of a children's show.

3

ANARCHY ROOLS OK

A TV had had a brilliant idea. They had decided on a new type of Saturday morning children's television programme; a kind of programme that would break away from the formality and politeness of the likes of *Blue Peter* – even an elephant disgracing itself in the middle of the *Blue Peter* studio did nothing to dent the presenters' reserve – and present a scene of studied anarchy of the type children delight in. It was to be called *Today Is Saturday, Watch And Smile*, or, as the presenters came to think of it, *Today Is Saturday, What A Shambles*. To the rest of the population, it was simply known as *Tiswas*.

When choosing the presenters for their new show, ATV executives showed a flair that almost amounted to genius. First up was John Asher, who turned into the straight man to

Chris's inspired lunacy. And then there was Tarrant himself, who was awarded £25 a week for appearing on the show – not bad money at the time. In his four years at ATV so far, he had shown himself to be a master of the unexpected. From early on Chris developed that urbane, relaxed, self-deprecating persona that was to stand him in such good stead in the future and it was the perfect attitude for the new show. Rarely fazed by anything and always able to see the funny side, Chris Tarrant was the obvious choice for *Tiswas*. 'I started giggling at interviews,' he later recalled, 'and it worked. They said, "You're young," and put me on *Tiswas*.'

The programme got off to an inauspicious start. At 10am on Saturday, July 5, 1974 the first programme, two and a half hours long and with a budget of £250, went on air to a Midlands audience – the rest of the country had to wait another two years to get involved. It was called *Today Is Saturday or the Tis-Was Show*. No one had ever seen anything like it. At that point it was still in the experimental stage: the producers had more or less decided to throw in everything they could think of that would appeal to children. This included cartoons, episodes of *Tarzan*, phone-ins (then unheard of), competitions, a group of children in the studio chatting to Tarrant plus a healthy dose of slapstick, gags and fooling around.

No one had expected much. The show had initially been allotted an eleven-week run: no one really expected it to survive much longer than that. But it did. As the series progressed, more and more viewers began to tune in, the presenters got bolder and Tarrant was elevated to equal status with Asher, with the two of them known as the 'Tiswas Twins'. The show itself came to be called simply Tiswas, it relocated to Studio 3 in the ATV complex in Birmingham and, when it came to the end of its run, it was deemed such a success that a full winter season was commissioned, starting on September 14, 1974.

Now Tiswas proper began. More presenters were brought in, including Peter Tomlinson, known as Poochie, Trevor East, ATV's head of sport and billed as Me, Myself, Yours Truly, 'Not The' Peter Matthews and Joan Palmer. The show continued to show film clips and cartoons, but the slapstick quota was upped considerably, as the producers began to realise it was what children wanted. It wasn't just children, either. Young adults loved it and, in the Midlands at least, were beginning to tune in right from the very beginning.

The studio audience had now risen to 50 and they also took the lunacy in good part, being handed out letters announcing, 'The company cannot be held responsible for any mishaps during transmission caused by stray pies or other scripted missiles.' However, in order to keep the relevant authorities satisfied – in this case the Independent Broadcasting Authority – there also had to be some serious or educational element as part of the programme, and so crusades were introduced: for water/road safety, for example, or for better play facilities. There was also the Tiswas Fascinating Fact File, designed both to amuse and to educate. The programme was by now compulsive viewing and the

100th edition was broadcast from the Hednesford Raceway, Cannock, in front of an audience of 30,000, with banger races supplying the lunatic element. Everyone loved it.

It was a slightly odd period in Tarrant's professional life for, to begin with, he found himself both as a serious news presenter and also as an anarchic children's television personality. Something had to give and it soon did. 'There was this really strange period for a year where I was doing the news Monday to Friday and *Tiswas* on Saturday with a bucket on my head and beans down my trousers,' said Chris. 'Understandably, ATV thought there was a real credibility gap. I'd say, "Good evening, 45 people have been killed in a bus crash," and everyone would start laughing. I decided to be a bucket person full time and I've never regretted it.'

By now, the buzz surrounding the show had started to seep out to the rest of the country and it was eventually snapped up by all of the ITV regions. By 1977 it was almost nationwide. In 1976 the BBC had begun broadcasting *Multi-Coloured Swap Shop* hosted by Noel Edmonds, but *Tiswas* held its own – the Rolling Stones to *Swap Shop*'s The Beatles. Tarrant, in particular, was really standing out. He was not afraid to take risks in front of the audience and that gave the show an edge. No one ever really knew what was about to happen.

'*Tiswas* had an anarchic feel, which really made an impact,' David Savage recalled on a website devoted to the show. 'On a basic level, one week the show would start and Tarrant would be tucking into egg and chips as he started hosting it, another he'd be washing his hair in a bowl of water

– at the time, one of very staid presentation, this was really something new and had the kind of impact you obviously couldn't reproduce nowadays. But there was also a genuine feel of improvisation and the show almost about to fall apart. A common catchphrase and obvious in-joke was, "We don't just throw this show together, you know," and it's apparently true that they didn't really rehearse and the cameraman never knew for sure what was coming next or what they were supposed to be doing.'

As the show's popularity soared, the line-up of presenters changed. ATV chose magnificently well. Some stayed only briefly, including Jim Davidson and Jasper Carrott, some stayed for years. These included a young black, little-known comedian called Lenworth J Henry who had recently won *New Faces*, the very glamorous and chirpy Sally James and two totally up-for-it types called John Gorman and Bob Carolgees. Numerous other cast members came and went, while the programme was now attracting guests of the calibre of Michael Palin and Spike Milligan.

Ironically, given how well they were to work together and, indeed, what great friends they later became, Tarrant was initially unhappy about having Sally James on the show. 'When I joined *Tiswas*, it was in its third year and the truth is that, if Chris had had his way, I would never have got the job,' Sally said. 'At that point it was an all-male team and Chris was aghast that they were going to bring in a girl. He thought that it was a very bad idea that I should infiltrate the male bastion that was *Tiswas*. Fortunately for me, the producers overruled him. Despite his reservations, we got on very well from the beginning.'

The chemistry between the two of them – and everyone else – provoked a brilliant sparkle of fun. By this time the whole nation (barring the odd ITV region) was lapping up the programme. Tarrant was by now the undisputed star of the show and was adept at siding with children rather than the adults: he would sit at a desk in the centre of the show, sometimes joined by Sally James, but, when he felt the action was flagging, he would lead the children in an attack on the caged adults present, hurling water and who knows what else.

The cage became one of the major features of the show. If you were an adult, it was the only way to get on the programme: you volunteered to be locked in for the duration, along with guest celebrities and the odd T-shirted woman, where, at Tarrant's whim, you would get buckets of water thrown over you, or perhaps gunk. One of the programme's many innovations was 'Wunda Gloo'.

On one occasion, John Peel, Rick Parfitt and several members of the rock band Rainbow were imprisoned in the cage, when someone lit up a joint. Tarrant, who might have been crazy, but certainly wasn't stupid – this was live children's television – promptly doused the cage with water, putting out the joint in the process. He has always refused to name the offender, but it might have been one of the members of Rainbow.

'When we did the cage, where adults sat and got pelted with food and water,' said Sally James, 'it was going to be there for one week but we got absolutely inundated with people who wanted to go in it. There were more adults wanting to go in the cage than kids wanting to go on the show. It unleashed a bit of madness in some people and there was no sign of the great British reserve.'

Lenworth, aka Lenny Henry, was also proving himself to be something of a star. He was beginning to shape some of his most popular impersonations, including Trevor 'McDoughnut' and Mr 'Grapple My Grapenuts' David Bellamy. Lenny was also creating original characters, something that would be a staple of his later career, including one wonderful persona, Algernon Winston Spencer Castlereagh Razzmatazz, whose greatest luxury was condensed milk. Bob Carolgees, a ventriloquist, briefly became a star through his Spit The Dog creation, an aggressive mongrel that spat at anyone in its firing range, while mayhem and custard pies remained a staple feature throughout.

The show had now become cult viewing amongst hungover adults, as well as children. It had such an impact that it actually changed pub-going habits, with Britons staying in to watch telly rather than going for a lunchtime pint. Tarrant later recalled its effect, while admitting that it was ironic that he, himself, would have been no good as a comedian. 'The show stopped Britain every Saturday for seven years,' he said. 'It was such a pull it killed off Saturday morning pictures. I can't tell a joke to save my life. I can never remember punchlines. I'm hopeless at that sort of thing. I can't sing, either. *Tiswas* was great fun and we made it up as we went along, but, if I had to tell jokes for a living, my family would starve.' ·

Chris was living hard. On one occasion friends on the show remember him staggering in on Friday night after an item about a brewery became an excuse for a party. His colleagues had to put him in the local Holiday Inn to sleep it off and then threw him in the swimming pool at 6am the following morning. Tarrant made a full recovery and presented the show as normal.

Everyone involved in the programme has nothing but happy memories of their time on *Tiswas*. Sally James remembers a wonderful era. 'I think the reason it was so successful was the team – we were such a little close-knit team, we all got on so well,' she said many years later. 'Plus, Chris didn't care who we upset – although he cared passionately about the programme – and that unleashed a lot of stuff. We just got rid of that "great British reserve". It was a funny way to earn a living; we'd get letters from the NSPCC saying it wasn't right for children to be pulled up by their ears, it was damaging them and all this crap – Chris'd be, like, two fingers to that and carry on.

'People still ring me probably once a month and ask me for a quote about the show or "What are you doing now?" or "What's your memory of *Tiswas*?" It's the same with Chris, even though he's gone on to do *Millionaire* – they still want to talk to him about *Tiswas*. Fifty-four per cent of our audience were over 18, which for a Saturday morning show was unusual; I think it changed Saturday morning TV – it wasn't then perceived to be just for children, it could be a family time.'

And, as it increased in popularity, more and more big names were clamouring to appear as guests. Cliff Richard, Madness, Elvis Costello all appeared, as did Robert Plant. 'Chris and I were sitting in a Holiday Inn one night having a drink,' said Sally, 'and Robert Plant came in and said, "Excuse me, I'm Robert Plant, any chance I could come on the programme?" Next day he was there, he got dressed up as a flower in Compost Corner, got a custard pie in his face and went off happy!'

It is difficult to overestimate the impact *Tiswas* had. On another occasion, Sally remembered how the show was put together and the hysteria that then developed around it. 'Every Saturday, Chris, Bob, John, Lenny and I made complete idiots of ourselves,' she said. 'We chucked buckets of water, dodged the custard pie-wielding Phantom Flan Flinger and rolled around in goo. We sang "Mule Train" while banging ourselves over the head with tin trays. We encouraged children to flan their teachers and we put their parents behind bars in our cage. First time around, everything we did attracted enormous attention.'

That was certainly true. Under the guise of the Four Bucketeers, Tarrant and co. released a record, the 'Bucket of Water Song'. It made it to number 26 in the charts on May 3, 1980 and led to an album and nationwide tour. Sally James remembers that too. 'Take our "Bucket of Water Song",' she said. 'We performed it one Saturday. The reaction was immediate: in pubs all over the country, people joined in, chucking whatever they could find over each other. What had we started? We decided to release a single, which sold thousands of copies and stayed in the charts for over six weeks. The thing is, *Tiswas* wasn't really a kids' show. *Tiswas* appreciation societies sprang up in dozens of pubs.

'So we toured universities and theatres, selling out wherever we went. The finale of our act was highly sophisticated. All electrics were removed from the stage, hundreds of buckets of water appeared and we launched into our hit song. The audience stormed to the front of the stage and, at appropriate moments in the song, we drenched them in water. It is a sight I will never forget. We had to swim out of some theatres and were banned from reappearing at others. At The Venue in Camden Town, the management told us, "We had The Clash here last week and they weren't as much trouble as you lot." Wimbledon Theatre sent us a bill for a new row of seats.'

The song itself, jolly as it was, couldn't really be called a work of art. Here is a sample of the lyrics:

We sing this song as we march along
We bash the cymbal and crash the gong
We sing the song, the bucket of water song ...

But no matter. Everyone loved it.

Tiswas became so big that all the 'serious' newspapers started analysing it, much to Tarrant's irritation, calling it anarchic, satirical, self-reverential. 'No it wasn't,' he protested years later. 'It really wasn't. There was this constant analysis of *Tiswas*. It wasn't like that. The in-depth articles I read about *Tiswas* were utterly wrong. I remember the *Guardian* or maybe the *Observer*, one of the loftier papers, did this thing about Lenny Henry throwing a pie in my face. "In that moment, Lenny was speaking out for 300 years of black oppression by the white man." No he wasn't, he comes from Dudley, he's a mate and he picked up a pie because there was one left.'

But, of course, as his fame spread, so the pressures mounted on Tarrant. One outlet was, of course, fishing. On Saturday afternoons, with *Tiswas* over for the week, Chris would head to the Birmingham fish market to buy bait and be greeted by all the stall holders. 'We used to have a huge wind-down after *Tiswas*,' Tarrant said years later, 'a long, long lunch, but I would end up thinking, I'm going fishing and I've got to go and buy my herrings and mackerel. And it'd be, "Oh hello, Tarrant, come over here, son, you know where the best herrings are." When I was in Birmingham last year I went in – and they were all there, the same lads. They were all a little bit older, a little bit balder and a little bit fatter round the middle, but they were like, "Hello, CT, come on over, me old son." I was in there for about two hours. It was brilliant; we had such a laugh.'

Bob Carolgees has equally happy memories of the programme, and its leading man. He isn't surprised that Chris is still such a success on TV. 'He's a genius,' he said. 'If he wasn't in the business, he'd have to be in a home. The way his mind works is amazing. He's so bright and sharp he can give you a reply almost before you've asked the question.'

Bob now runs a candle shop in Frodsham, Cheshire, but remembers the *Tiswas* days very fondly. 'It was manic, but we had a good laugh,' he said. 'As far as we were concerned we weren't making it for kids, we were making it for adults waking up with hangovers.' He remembers the outrage that the show caused when it was finally shown in London.

'London was one of the last places to get it, although it had been going for years in other parts of the country,' he said. 'Suddenly somebody noticed the viewing figures and dropped Bill Oddie and his *Saturday Banana* and put us on in London instead. But Fleet Street didn't realise it wasn't a new show and was outraged by this programme with a spitting dog and people getting covered in gunge. The next week the papers were full of calls for it to be banned, but when they realised that it had been on for years and everybody loved it they changed their minds and the next week it was the best thing since sliced bread.'

The gradual pace with which *Tiswas* took over the country's Saturday mornings allowed its presenters time to develop their unique brand of madness, according to Carolgees. 'That slow burn was ideal because it let us do what we wanted,' he said. 'We made mistakes and we learned from them and we got better. The problem with Saturday morning TV these days is that people are trying to recreate that spontaneity, but you can't be spontaneous if you've been rehearsing everything.'

Of course, this was the era of punk rock and anarchy was the great fashion of the times. Even so, *Tiswas* stood out not just from other children's television programmes but from anything that had ever appeared on TV. And it is difficult to overestimate quite how much influence that programme had. It introduced the concept of 'Zoo TV' to Britain, the kind of television where anything could happen and usually did, where the audience was invited to participate and where the presenter comes across as a quirky figure, out to disrupt the status quo and at odds with the establishment. Chris Tarrant was that figure back in the days of *Tiswas* and his influence stretches right up to the present day. Chris Evans's television shows, although not aimed at children, are direct descendants of the pioneering styles taken back then.

TFI Friday broke all the rules – but then so did *Tiswas*, which, amongst an awful lot else, featured 'The Quiet Bits', when Chris got serious for the sake of the IBA, 'Telly Selly Time', i.e. advertisements, 'Underates', a deliberately misspelled competition for smaller viewers, the 'Phantom Flan Flinger' (someone dressed up as Darth Vader who went around flinging flans) and 'The Welly Phone', two wellies tied together as a prop phone. None of those would have been out of place on *TFI Friday*. Chris Tarrant, incidentally, is dismissive of his namesake and it's obvious why – he was doing it all a good 20 years before his rival got in on the act.

Tiswas was the making of Tarrant. Although he didn't achieve quite the household-name status he has now, it was widely known within the industry that he was responsible for this ground-breaking new format – and that it was he who showed that presenters on children's television could make the crossover into the adult market. He also made children's programming far more important within the overall television output and, in so doing, stole a march on the people who'd had a virtual monopoly on the genre, the BBC.

'I think Chris Tarrant was a pioneer,' said Brian MacLaurin of MacLaurin PR, which represents Chris. 'You have to remember that he actually started out as a news reporter in the Midlands, but managed to sell an idea for a Saturday morning show that he wrote and produced himself, so it was dirt cheap. Before that, there wasn't really a Saturday morning youth market as we've come to know it now.'

It was an amazing time for everyone involved, but took its toll on Tarrant's personal life. He and Sheila had got married in 1974, just as *Tiswas* was taking off, and had two daughters, Helen and Jennifer. The family was living in an idyllic little cottage in Langley, Warwickshire, but, as Chris grew increasingly successful, he also grew increasingly neglectful, as he himself would come to admit. He drank 'a swimming pool of whisky' when Helen was born, he once said. He had always expected to be deferred to by other girlfriends and now the same was proving true with Sheila. 'The marriage was also difficult because I married at 28 and a year later started doing *Tiswas* and became famous,' he recalled. 'Young girls would come up to me in clubs and blatantly proposition me in front of my wife, which is impossible to live with.'

Tarrant was drinking extremely heavily and Sheila began to suspect that there might be other women on the horizon. There were rumours about Tarrant and his co-presenter, which, while untrue, did nothing to help matters. The situation worsened and in 1981, at the height of *Tiswas*'s success, the pair split up. Tarrant promptly went a little mad, smoking up to 60 cigarettes a day, drinking even more heavily and ploughing his way through the many women who were only too happy to succumb to his charms.

It was a very acrimonious split and, years later, Sheila told of her misery within the marriage. 'Chris had always been a heavy drinker, but it got progressively worse during those *Tiswas* days,' she said. 'Sometimes he wouldn't come home for days on end because he was out boozing. I've watched him get through a bottle of Scotch in a day. He'd sit down at his typewriter at ten in the morning to write a programme script and start slugging back the Scotch.

'He's always been very high-handed, arrogant and had a vicious temper – and drink just made it worse. I knew when he was on a bender to stay out of his way because he could be very aggressive. He never laid a finger on me, but I was scared of him. He's a big man and would throw things around the house when he was drunk. It was very scary.'

Clearly, the situation was escalating out of control. On one occasion, Tarrant nearly managed to set fire to the cottage. 'The kitchen was full of smoke,' Sheila said. 'The idiot had put some bacon under the grill then slumped comatose, face down on the kitchen table. Another night, I was woken up by a phone call from a woman I didn't even know. She said she'd been drinking with Chris and her husband and then had a row. Later she turned up at the house. She was surprised to see me pregnant. Chris clearly hadn't told her he was going to be a dad.' Tarrant himself arrived back shortly afterwards, held up by two policemen. 'They'd found him slumped not far from the house,' said Sheila. 'He was always very good at dismissing these things and accused me of being a nag.'

Perhaps the worst occasion for Sheila was when she had just given birth to their first daughter, Helen. Tarrant arrived at the hospital drunk, with a blonde woman in tow. 'Chris was lurching and slurring and effing and blinding,' said Sheila. 'It was awful.'

Sheila recalls a very different Tarrant from the one known to the vast majority of people, but his newfound success had gone to his head. He was to come back down to earth with a bump, but for a while made that colossal mistake of believing in his own publicity, which brought out his worst side. Sheila privately called him Tarrant the Tyrant and complained that, despite the money that was beginning to pour in, little of it came in her direction. 'Chris had a very black side,' she said. 'As well as his short temper, he could be very mean. I once asked him to buy a washing machine, but he never got round to it.'

Matters finally came to a head when Sheila's father Robert died in 1982 and Chris was unable to offer her any support. 'When I told him I wanted a divorce, all he could say was, "You're not getting your hands on my money."' It was clearly a miserable period for everyone involved.

Tarrant himself looks back on the period with a great deal of regret. 'I succeeded in messing up four lives,' he said 15 years later. 'We should have been a very happy, contented family unit, like Ingrid and I are now with our two kids. But I buggered it up by getting the proportions of home life and TV life wrong. I've always regretted it. I just wish we had all stayed together.'

Tarrant paid maintenance and child support and kept in touch with his two daughters, but also went on to feel a great deal of guilt where they were concerned. 'I wish I knew in my first marriage what I know now,' he said in the mid-1990s. 'I wasn't the best dad in the world to Helen and Jennifer. I've said to them quite openly that I know I wasn't. When they were tiny, my career was just taking off. I was producing and hosting *Tiswas* and it was occupying me full time, seven days a week, seven nights a week. I just wasn't at home much, which I still feel guilty about to this day.'

Back then, though, Chris threw himself into the single life with a vengeance. He was approaching his mid-30s, but it almost seemed as if he was trying to make up for missing out on all the wildness of the 1960s. He embraced wine, women and song with gusto, throwing himself into the lifestyle.

Tarrant started his new life by moving to a house near Stratford-upon-Avon, buying a Mercedes and getting up most days at 5am to go fishing. After that came work and after that came women – lots of them. 'I worked all the time, which is the classic way of running away,' said Chris. 'I also went out with lots of women and became a terrible liar. I was an unfaithful Jack the lad. It was a game I should have played at 18, which I played at 30. I didn't approve of myself and in retrospect I think it was really stupid.'

His life became increasingly aimless outside of work. 'I drank a lot, maybe 20 pints a night,' he said years later. 'But when you've split from your wife and kids and you're suddenly single, what do you do? You go down to the pub, don't you? I spent a lot of time in public houses and things. I just had to see this terrible business through, really, sort of resolve things in my own head a bit. I was doing my show *OTT* at the time and, in trying to cope, I really did go over the top at times. The question of divorce came up during the series. I thought, Oh well, I'll just get through the series and everything will be OK. But when the series was over, it was too late. We were too far apart, and too much damage had been done to mend bridges.

'As for the sex, it was companionship. I just needed somebody there with me, beside me. I was 30-something, in the public eye, and there were always girls available for someone in my position. I'm not proud of that part of my life. I'll tell you just how pointless it became. One day I made love to four women and it meant nothing to me at all. It was just a stupid part of a rather weak period in my life. I'm amazed at rock 'n' rollers who are still doing that stuff. I wouldn't get any pleasure from it, added to which it's bloody dangerous.

'For me, it was just an aberration, a phase, a knee-jerk reaction to the pain I felt inside. It's certainly not something I'd ever brag about. It was horrible, actually, not a lot of fun. I used to go to parties where girls would be having it off on the sofa with blokes they didn't know, and doing it in front of everybody, because that was their kick. I remember going to a party which turned into a free for all, a real orgy. There were stunning women there for the taking – and I just sort of rather pathetically went home. I thought, I don't want to do this in front of lots of other people. I just don't like that sort of thing.'

On another occasion, Tarrant was accused of boasting about sleeping with four women in one day. His reply was typically self-deprecating. 'I didn't sleep with them,' he said. 'I stayed awake. Sleeping never got you into trouble. I'm not proud of it, although it was a bloody good day. Several girls have asked if they were one of the four. They all said, "If I was, I must have been the last because you weren't very good." I'm not a macho superstud. I did at 30 what I should have done at 17. Having been at public school, I had a lot of catching up to do. I was skint when I divorced. 1981 was a very rough year. I hung on to my home in Warwickshire by the good nature of the bank manager. I was bloody lucky I never stopped working.'

One person who remained immensely sympathetic to Tarrant through the whole period was his own father, Basil. 'When his first marriage broke up, he was absolutely shattered,' he said, 'but he managed to carry on working and didn't shirk his responsibilities as a father. In the depths of winter, he'd finish working in London and jump into the car to drive to Stratford to take the children out for meals.'

It turned into a miserable time not only personally but professionally. Tarrant is now so successful that it is often forgotten he's had his fair share of failure as well. By the beginning of the 1980s, he'd been with *Tiswas* for seven years and was getting restless. It was time for a new project and so he left *Tiswas*, which survived for only one more season without him – and took a big risk with his career.

4

IT REALLY WAS OTT

The thinking was simple. The massively popular *Tiswas* had as big a following amongst adults as it did amongst children – so why not go the whole hog and produce a kind of *Tiswas* specifically for adults? It couldn't fail, was the reasoning, and so came about the birth of *OTT*, short for Over The Top. The trouble was, it lived up to its moniker.

Where to start on the disaster that was *OTT*? Was it the naked men dancing around with nothing to cover their modesty except balloons? Was it the features that saw more men shoving rats down their trousers? Was it the topless women jiggling around for what seemed to be no other reason than being topless? Or perhaps it was just not well written enough. It featured the likes of Lenny Henry – now shining much earlier in the evening in the excellent and popular show *Three Of A Kind* – and Alexei Sayle, but neither really showed much flair. To put it bluntly, it was a terrible show, right from the start.

The real problem was the lack of boundaries. *Tiswas* revelled in its own anarchy, but it was still a children's show, which meant that some lines could not be overstepped. *OTT*, however, felt that it could do what it liked – and so it did, regardless of whether it was actually amusing or necessary. And that lack of discipline extended through into the material. Perhaps if, in between topless women and balloon-clad men, the show had been genuinely ground breaking, it would have worked. But it wasn't.

Once up and running, there were scores of complaints. The audience simply didn't like it. And it was proving a problem in other ways as well. In 1982 ITV looked set to be revitalised by the introduction of three new franchises: Central, TSW and TVS. *OTT* went out just before 11pm on Saturday evenings on Central – and its debut came on Central's second day of broadcasting.

Indeed, the programme was initially promoted as the jewel in Central's crown, with a budget of £250,000 – massively higher than that of *Tiswas*. However, warning signs were there from the start. 'The show is so up to date, the team is still working on its formula, if indeed it has one,' said Alan Kennaugh of Central TV. 'But it will definitely feature plenty of splash and splosh in the children's tradition, with characters like Count Custard throwing his pies around.' Warning bells should have been ringing loud and clear. No clear formula and a custard-pie flinger in what was supposed to be a ground-breaking show – no wonder it turned out so bad.

But no one saw the iceberg up ahead, least of all Tarrant, who was responsible for the show. 'We know it has enormous potential appeal for adults,' he said. Everyone else agreed. '*Tiswas* was marvellous to work on,' said Lenny Henry. 'It was a new style of lunatic humour and we got away with murder. When I first started *Tiswas*, my nerves used to go before each show simply because it was live. But now, in *OTT*, I just get on with it.' But significantly Lenny failed to get his new partner, Dawn French, to come on to the show – because she didn't think it was funny enough.

Tarrant had, himself, a couple of years earlier unwittingly laid a finger on one of the problems he was now encountering, when he pointed out that he was not a comedian – and yet, here he was, trying to write a funny show. In fairness, though, he could certainly spot talent in others. It is a sign of the wasted opportunity that was *OTT*, in that it was the first programme to feature Alexei Sayle on television and it also discovered Helen Atkinson-Wood and Colette Hiller. And yet the show was an unmitigated disaster.

Tarrant himself enjoyed it. He later confessed that his favourite ever stunt in any programme he made was when he put 20 tax inspectors in a cage on the show and threw custard at them. It was plainly trying to recreate the anarchy of the cage in *Tiswas* but just didn't have the same amusement value. Even Chris was upset when the model Julia Humphries suddenly and unexpectedly took her top off on live TV – 'The phones were jammed within seconds,' he conceded. 'I was just as shocked – I thought she had a bra on underneath her clothes.'

And there were rows behind the scenes – big ones. There was a massive upset when Colette Hiller told Tarrant the band had come on too early – 'OK, Colette,' Tarrant replied to the astonished actress, 'next time you write the fucking running order.' Abrasive Tarrant was still in full swing.

Nor was he very pleased when people tried to give him a dose of his own medicine. Tarrant was having a quiet drink in a pub once, when someone suddenly poured a pint over him, yelling, 'It's *Tiswas* Torrential Time!' Unsurprisingly, Chris went ballistic and made for the fellow. 'I was that mad I had to be held off him,' he said later. 'But I ended up buying him a drink.' The divorce and the bad reviews were clearly getting to him. Tarrant has never been labelled a difficult man to work with and he is usually affability itself to his public – but everyone has a breaking point and he was clearly nearing his.

In 1982, the well-known television commentator Chris Dunkley summed up what was wrong with the programme. 'My own objection to *OTT* is twofold: it is not funny enough and it emasculates those who are funny,' he wrote. 'Chris Tarrant has an attractively offhand attitude about the mystique of television and an engagingly laidback style of presenting the whole thing, yet the entire show seems dreadfully contrived, perhaps because everyone works so hard at the spontaneity. We know from *Three Of A Kind* that Lenny Henry has a wonderfully original comedy style, but the material written for him in *OTT* isn't good enough. He tries to compensate with "funny" hats and "funny" voices which are so unfunny they make you wince.

'Worst of all is the effect upon Alexei Sayle. When I went to see him live in Soho he made me laugh so much I fell off my seat and banged my chin on the one in front. *OTT* manages to convey about half his true frenzy and none of his bite. He can be the most startling comedian since Lenny Bruce, but that will not come across on television because, whatever the telephone complainers may believe, television is the least permissive of our mass media.'

In fact, Sayle was to discover the right vehicle for him on television that same year when he went on to feature in *The Young Ones*. He was also the first to leave *OTT*, sensing that it was not going to last, only to be replaced by Bernard Manning. One Sunday, a vicar told his congregation there would be no service that day – instead an hour-long prayer that Central TV take *OTT* off the air. Tarrant himself, however, was bemused by the critics' hostility to the show, especially as the audience figures were so good.

'The Watchdogs of Worship used to ring me every ten minutes for a year,' he said. 'Ken, who put rats down his tights, got a lot of complaints. Yes, it was gross, but offensive? We actually succeeded in making the British public feel sorry for rats. I don't understand why there was all this fuss. One woman wrote to say she was so disgusted, she had to send her five-year-old daughter to bed. The show went out at midnight. I'm quietly proud of *OTT*. They should have done a second series. Ahh, it's only a bit of telly. It ain't that important.'

It took years before the feeling of shock and hurt and the show's abrupt demise wore off. In 1995, more than a decade after it disappeared from our screens, Tarrant was still brooding. 'I felt very disappointed, very let down,' he said of Central's decision to pull the programme. 'The show had actually been hugely popular in its way. Central now keep asking me to give permission for a "golden-moments-of" compilation, but I always say no. Stuff them.'

However, as the years passed, Tarrant began to see where it all went wrong. 'The balloon men were a mistake, maybe,' he said in 1999. 'And the man who put rats down his tights, that was a definite blunder.' On one occasion, Ken ended up kicking the rat – another low point. 'The switchboard was red hot after him. One man said, "Those magnificent animals should be free to roam the sewers and should not be forced down any man's trousers." But the guy eating his brains with a spoon I thought was tremendous.'

But it was a blow and, ironically, Chris was to suffer far more than almost everyone else involved. Lenny Henry had *Three Of A Kind*, Alexei Sayle had *The Young Ones* and the new discoveries soon began making a mark for themselves but for Tarrant, the most closely involved in the whole fiasco, it was a disaster. Meanwhile, in the background, the divorce was grinding on, as Chris himself drank ever more heavily and engaged in one pointless fling after another.

Many years later he recalled the miserable time – and how it resulted in him having a lucky charm. 'About 20 years ago, everything was going wrong,' he said. 'I was going through a rough divorce and the critics were panning *OTT*. One night in Birmingham, I heard this shout as I was walking along and I thought, Blimey, I'm in big trouble here. But this lad, aged about 20, said, "Hey, man, I like what you do, take this," and he hands me this silver sixpence. Three months later my career changed for the better and my private life perked up. I'd like to meet that guy again to thank him. He changed my life.'

In fact, throughout his career, Tarrant has just about never been out of work. But for some years to come he was to maintain a lower profile than he had during the *Tiswas* years – and in the industry many speculate that, in some ways, the cancellation of *OTT* was the making of him. It was such a shock, industry experts argue, that it induced a work ethic that has lasted the rest of his life. Tarrant himself refutes this, but it certainly explains why, in his 50s, he catches four hours of sleep a night, rises at 5am to do a gruelling morning show, works until about midnight, indulges his love of fishing and still, somewhere, makes time to be with his family. For such a laidback character, Tarrant often gives the impression of being a very driven man.

A year later, Chris launched another show, *Saturday Stayback*, an *OTT*-style spin off, that lasted only six episodes despite yet more discoveries: Tony Slattery and Phil Cool. Some of the old crowd from *OTT* and *Tiswas* were there as well and again an attempt was made to create an adult version of *Tiswas*, but it failed for many of the same reasons. It was also not without incident. On one occasion the team attracted the attention of the police, who saw lights on in the Dog Inn at Warley in the West Midlands. Suspecting out-of-hours drinking – this was well before the current free-for-all – they burst in, only to find Chris and his team in rehearsals.

Indeed, throughout the years, it has often been suggested that, rather than trying to remake *Tiswas*, the show itself should be resurrected, complete with its original presenters. Thankfully, wiser counsel has prevailed. Sally James has sensibly said that *Tiswas* is best left as a memory.

Tarrant himself said, 'They kept talking about bringing it back and in 1990 they even asked me if I would like to do it again, but I've had enough. I don't want to spend another second of my life with beans down my pants or pies in my ears.' It was a sensible decision. About the only television show ever to repeat its early success after a gap of nearly two decades is Michael Parkinson's talk show – and in that case it didn't matter that the presenter was not as young as he once was.

And so began a slightly calmer time. Tarrant continued to work, albeit in more low-profile roles, which he credits as the key to his longevity in the media. Some people thought he should have done something really subversive after *Tiswas*: the man himself did not. 'I've never been about bringing down governments,' he said.

'This is all about having a bit of a crack. I've never had a plan. People have never understood that about me, but I think it's why I've survived. I've never been into the politics of television and the power games the idiots in charge of this industry play. If you go around thinking they are going to sack you, you might just give them the idea to do it. In 25 years I've never been sacked and, by any standards, that's pretty amazing.' It is a very wise philosophy and one that has stood him in good stead.

And so Chris continued to do what he was best at: getting on with the public. He presented *Hotline*, a live phone-in programme based on a French offering, in which viewers rang in with a problem: the need to find a dance partner, for instance, or trace lost holiday snaps. Other viewers were then meant to ring in with a solution. Chris Dunkley didn't think too much of this one, either.

'The trouble with an opening programme of this sort,' he said, 'is that you clearly cannot afford to risk there being no response and so the mystery object which had supposedly been residing in Gloria Hunniford's drawers for years and was produced at the start was oh-so-conveniently identified at the end by the arrival in the studio of a young man with the object displayed on a live chicken's beak.

'And the two ladies *d'un* certain age looking for dancing partners were met by two men of the right age who just happened to get to the studio wearing nice suits and fresh haircuts to partner them. And somehow Chris Tarrant knew that the "chance" caller ringing about a gramophone record cigarette card possessed the ancient equipment to play it on and so on and so on. Apart from the people looking for unidentified holiday snaps (who received no calls whatever) the whole gallimanfry was as phoney as all get out.' Well – at least it paid the rent.

Tarrant's life now verged on the bizarre. In 1983, he presented 'Miss Lovely Legs' on Brighton beach. 'Right in the middle of the competition,' he recalled, 'this loony walked in with a shopping bag and insisted on parading around with the rest of the girls. He was a dead ringer for Frank Spencer.'

He was still running around with a lot of women and, apart from when he spent time with his daughters, had no domestic life to speak of. 'I can cook a great English breakfast,' he said at the time. 'The hard part is making sure the whole lot is swimming in grease. Most of the time I eat out. I love Greek food and steaks and lashings of alcohol – anything as long as it kicks like a mule.'

Asked about his vices, he replied, 'The usual ones: boozing, women, that sort of thing. But my biggest addiction is fishing. I usually get up at 5am every day and go out with my rods for a couple of hours before driving into London.' And his love life? 'That's rather complicated. Now that I'm divorced, I desperately try to spend as much time as possible with my daughters Helen and Jennifer. There are a number of other ladies in my life, as well as a donkey and a goat.'

A whole series of programmes followed. Tarrant did a three-month stint on *TV-am*, which had been launched amidst much fanfare on February 1, 1983. The programme was called *Good Morning Britain* and had a shaky start: David

Frost was an early presenter, but was soon replaced by Nick Owen, who worked alongside Anne Diamond. Bad ratings early on in the show meant that Greg Dyke, now head of the BBC, was called in to take matters in hand: this he did by introducing a character called Roland Rat.

You would have thought that Tarrant would be one of the star presenters in the middle of all this, but he wasn't. Returning very briefly to his early roots, he was mainly a newsreader and was such a peripheral figure in the drama that surrounded those early days on the station that people often forget he was there at all. Other slots included 'zany' reports from around the country, such as the time he kicked a sumo wrestler in the stomach on Blackpool beach one morning, brightly announcing, 'I think I'll just call him "sir" for the rest of the morning!' It was dispiriting stuff.

And the hours were almost too much even for him. His wake-up call was brought forward to 3.30am, not least because he had to spend time in hair and make-up. 'That was even worse,' he said, after he joined Capital. 'At least on radio it does not matter how you look. At *TV-am* you have to spend an hour before the show having your make-up put on – and deciding which of Anne Diamond's frocks to wear today!'

Tarrant also compiled a book on trivia to help make ends meet. His expenses, after all, were high: he was supporting his ex-wife and two children, maintaining two establishments, running a fairly expensive lifestyle and travelling all over the country. Television is a well-paid medium and Chris certainly wasn't badly off, but he was nowhere near as wealthy as he is today – nor, at that stage, did it look as if he would ever be.

It was a sobering experience and only strengthened Tarrant's determination to succeed. 'He was doing inserts on this crummy breakfast programme after having had his own show and Lenny Henry was sky high at that point,' said a colleague who worked with him at Capital Radio. 'It really hit him: he became tough. He began to hate his rivals.' Tarrant, of course, would not agree with this analysis – but he remains very aware that to hang in as long as he has is unusual.

He quite frequently talks about the longevity of his career and how surprising it is to him as much as anyone else that he's still around. But it was at this testing stage of his career that Tarrant showed the qualities that were to carry him through. He was not grand, he did the work that was available and he didn't complain about his circumstances. He simply got on with the job.

More easily forgettable programmes followed. As Tarrant once said later, when everything had picked up, 'I was working steadily, but the career was a bit thin.' He went on to take over *TV-am*'s Saturday show, *Good Morning Britain*. *Lose A Million* and *The Main Event* followed and were quickly forgotten. He also did a season presenting *Cluedo*, which even he admitted was nonsense. 'The dullest experience ever,' he said. 'The producers kept telling me not to be silly. This was serious. It was courtroom drama. But the whole premise was ludicrous. There were six characters in the show and six episodes in each series. So, if Reverend Green had not done it by the end of episode five, you knew he would be next week. That always struck me as highly absurd.'

That was not all he had to say about it. Asked in later years what was the worst show he'd ever done, he immediately replied, '*Cluedo*. It was absolute garbage. It would take forever to film just a few lines because the audience had to be turned over to stop them getting bedsores. Richard Wilson, Rula Lenska, Koo Stark and I would get drunk and depressed about it every night in the hotel.'

The middle-of-the-road television rolled on. Next up was a programme called *Prove It*, in which people had to live up to their boasts. Tarrant himself kicked off the show by claiming that going to university had made him the lunatic he is today. 'Philosophy was the oddest thing,' he said. 'Do you know that all philosophy lecturers are completely mad? They've all got really grubby suits and spiky hair. Our bloke said, "Good morning, gentlemen, a new term. I want you all to consider the curtain on that window there." After an hour of complete silence, he said, "Thank you, gentlemen, I think you'll agree – a very good morning's work," and just walked out. Completely mad.'

He went on to talk about being forced to learn Anglo Saxon, which he considered to be a waste of time. 'Latin was equally stupid,' he went on. 'The masters would say, "Don't worry, Tarrant, you'll thank me one day." And 25 years later, I've still got no reason to thank anyone for a single word of Latin. I mean, all those wonderful conversational phrases like,

"Have you seen the spears of my brother?" I never found any use for it at all. When I eventually took up teaching, I was put in charge of a load of tough skinheads in south London. They were basically illiterate. They couldn't handle English, let alone Anglo Saxon or Latin.'

Prove It was an odd show. It featured British eccentrics, in one case bizarre inventions made by an inventor called John Ward, such as the Backpack Snow Machine – 'You can always have a White Christmas – just strap it on your back and spew out polystyrene snow storms as you go.' Another was the Dance Tutor, a frame that fitted round a couple of dancers, holding a chart with dance steps at eye level. This actually worked.

There was also the Personal Head Shampooer, perfect for bald men, as it was a little miniature carwash built around your choice of chair, with two furry pink pads to polish the head. And, finally, there was the Ultimate Television, with a windscreen wiper to clear the screen of flies, a gas ring on top to make the tea and something that swung across the gas ring to make the toast. It was television, Jim, but not as we know it.

There followed the likes of *Everybody's Equal*, in which Chris himself was once made to suffer – after he claimed to detest yuppies, especially estate agents, he was forced to take on a 200-strong audience of, you guessed it, estate agents. Funnily enough, *Everybody's Equal*, which was based on a French format, had a number of features that later appeared in *Who Wants To Be A Millionaire*. It involved contestants faced with questions and four multiple choice answers, in which speed of reply was almost as important as accuracy and in which, at the finale, contestants were asked to put a series of events in order.

Described at the time as 'one of the more inventive quizzes that ITV has done', the format went as follows. Questions were read out to a studio audience of 200, each of whom had a keypad, which provided four alternative answers. They had ten seconds to answer and everyone who got the question wrong – sometimes just one hapless individual, on whom the camera focused – was out. This continued until there were only ten people left. If, however, there were more than ten left after the sixth question, then the fastest ten to answer went through.

Round two was similar, except with four questions, and the person who answered the fourth question fastest went to the final round. They would then have to put four items in order – as did the audience – and, if they did so, they won £2,000. If they failed, the £2,000 was split between audience members who got it right. The format was by no means perfect: on one memorable occasion, 30 people had been knocked out, leaving 170 in the ring. Out of that 170, 166 got the next question wrong, which meant that round one ended immediately and round two began. 'I still remember Chris Tarrant trying desperately to fill the time,' said one viewer. The show ran for two seasons and, while it is a long way from *Millionaire*, it perhaps sowed a few ideas in Tarrant's flaxen-haired head. It also sparked interest from the United States, which was particularly heartening for the producers as the process tends to work the other way round.

Times were slowly improving. Tarrant was able to splash out on a new £600,000 home in Esher, Surrey, while still keeping the place in Warwickshire. His profile was growing too, as he became a stalwart at showbiz charity functions, such as a fishing match that raised £30,000 for Cancer Research. Although still most famous for *Tiswas*, he had by now definitely made the leap in the public perception from children's television presenter to adult television presenter – now all he needed was a great big show. And that, for now, continued to elude him.

But there were many compensations. By now Tarrant had discovered that he could significantly increase his income by doing voice-overs for commercials. And so a very lucrative side career began with Tarrant, amongst others things, advertising the Honey Monster's cereal. 'I'm not telling you how much I get for the ads, but I spend a lot of my evenings doing them,' he said. Whatever it was, it must have been good – the going rate back then was about £5,000 a go.

But he certainly hadn't lost the talent to irritate people. On an episode of *Through The Keyhole*, in which Tarrant regularly took part, presenter Loyd Grossman was taking viewers through the Humberside-based home of CND president Bruce Kent, when Chris noticed a plaque from Goole town council. He would rather spend six weeks in Wakefield High Security wing, said Chris, than take a holiday in the Humberside town. He then went on to call the townsfolk 'Goolies'. The usual furore ensued, with Goole's mayor, amongst others, standing up to complain.

Unmoved, Tarrant went on to have another go at estate agents. Asked what he would wish for in the 1989 Budget, he announced, 'I'd reduce income tax to 25 per cent across the board – except for estate agents, who I would tax at 150 per cent.' But, given that much of the rest of the country agreed with him, this time there was no outcry.

Chris continued with his advertising work, which was becoming increasingly profitable and in some ways more successful than his mainstream television career. He was now doing voice-overs for Hitachi, Toilet Duck and Orangina, while fronting yet another television series, *PSI*, which was to be shown on weekday afternoons, i.e. not on prime-time television. The work was steady, Chris was doing well but, as far as television was concerned, there was still no indication that Tarrant would ever be able to recreate the glory days of *Tiswas*.

PSI, which stood for Psychology, Slander and Intuition and which was based on a board game popular back in the mid-1980s, was huge at the time: it had spawned not only a television spin-off but a book as well. It was the brainchild of advertising copywriter Steve Knight, who not only developed the board game, but managed to sell the idea to US game giants Milton Bradley. 'It's a good excuse for talking about everyone's favourite person – themselves!'

The idea was simple: two teams of celebrities would compete to guess the identity of a mystery guest. However, to do so they had to compare the guests to objects – from cars to famous buildings, beer to olive oil. 'It can be hilarious,' said Chris, who was himself described as a cross between a polar bear, a Range Rover and a lemon meringue pie.

The show turned out to be popular, with papers queuing up to describe *PSI* in their own terms. For example, the *Daily Express* said that, if this game were a person, it would be a master of intrigues – like John le Carre. If it were a car, it would have hidden reserves of speed – like a Peugeot 205. All the usual suspects came on the show: to pick at random, guests included Christopher Biggins, Sue Cook, the late Kenny Everett, Vicki Michelle, Nicholas Parson and Su Pollard.

After two seasons, the programme changed its title to the more obvious *Celebrity Intuition* and, while its presenter remained, on television terms, in the middle league, it propelled its creator, Steve Knight, straight into the big league. On the back of the success of the show, Steve and his writing partner Mike Whitehill first started as freelancers, supplying material to, amongst others, Ken Dodd, Frankie Howerd and Hale and Pace. Then they really started running, supplying the script for Glenn Close and Mel Gibson at the Oscars. With *PSI*, they established an enduring relationship with Celador Productions, leading to two *Canned Carrott* series with the comedian Jasper Carrott, four *Carrott's Commercial Breakdown* specials and five series of *The Detectives*, amongst a good deal more.

As for Tarrant – on television, he seemed to be stuck in a rut of afternoon game shows, quizzes and competitions. One journalist coined the phrase 'to Tarrant' – i.e. to host any show at all, no matter how bad it is. He was ubiquitous without having any one great television success to his name – apart, of course, from *Tiswas*. He could so easily have continued in the nether regions of television – a fairly well-known face among daytime television viewers, but never in the major league, never one of the masters of the universe in television terms.

Tarrant himself spoke gamely about the situation, saying that in his first marriage the work/life balance had got out of control and he was determined that that would never happen again but, even so, he must have reflected a little bit on the injustice of it all. If you experience massive popularity on television in your late 20s and early 30s and then lose it by your 40s, life can sometimes seem tough. Indeed, because of his youthful appearance, not many people realised that by this time Tarrant was well into his 40s and middle-aged years.

But two things saved him. In the mid-1980s, Chris had taken on a new role, which he absolutely loved – as a radio presenter on Capital Radio. He was a natural at it and a massive success. On top of that, the stint at *TV-am* had proven to be worth it after all. For it was there that he met an attractive Norwegian-born television reporter with a vivacity to match his own. She was called Ingrid Dupré – and she was to become his second wife.

5

NOW WE ARE TWO

It was 1983 and Ingrid Dupré, a glamorous producer on *Good Morning Britain* was watching the television monitor in the newsroom. Much to her bemusement, a flaxen-haired reporter appeared to be struggling with a large animal. 'There was this guy in pink jeans lying on the ground underneath an elephant,' Ingrid recalled, 'and I just thought, what sort of people are *TV-am* giving jobs to? Someone said, "It's Chris Tarrant," and I replied, "Who the hell is Chris Tarrant?" He was meant to be quite famous – but I reckoned, if I didn't know him, he couldn't be that famous.'

It was an inauspicious start to what was to become the most important relationship in Tarrant's life. But at that stage, neither of them had a clue what was going to happen. Chris was still in his drinking and womanising phase and marrying again was the last thing on his mind. Ingrid was equally disillusioned. Like Chris, she was divorced with two small children, Dexter, four, and ten-month-old Fia, and she had no intention of tying the knot again. Her ex-husband, Tony Walsh, a TV cameraman, had been serially unfaithful and Ingrid had been badly hurt.

'I didn't believe in marriage any more,' she said. 'We'd broken up over his infidelity. One of his exes wrote to me, heartbroken, because he'd ended their relationship. I couldn't believe it and told him, "I don't want to end up as pen-pal to one of your exes."'

And so the couple split and Ingrid got on with her career. But it wasn't long before she bumped into her fellow reporter and the attraction between them was immediate. 'She immediately registered,' said Tarrant. 'She was wearing a brown tank suit thing. An all-in-one thingy, like a car mechanic. That's what she looked like, a gorgeous blonde Norwegian car mechanic.'

Initially, the two simply started sparring with one another – which they do to this day. But that is often a sign of two people fancying one another silly and not wanting to admit it – the same is true of Beatrice and Benedict in Shakespeare's *Much Ado About Nothing* – and so it proved to be in this case.

'One of our first arguments was over a lobster,' Ingrid recalled. 'Chris insisted live lobsters were a deep red colour, I insisted they were bluey-black and only turned red when they were cooked. I bet him £20 I was right. I phoned someone at Billingsgate fish market and put them on to Chris. I remember him shouting, "No, mate – you've got it wrong. You are definitely not right." He never paid me the £20 – but it's accumulating with interest.' Tarrant had quite clearly met his match.

Ingrid Dupre was one of five children born in Norway, but she and her family ended up in Hertfordshire. After leaving school she began a career in fashion design, but switched her energies to creating a successful export business before opening her own shop on the Kings Road in Chelsea. At the same time she worked freelance for ITN, co-ordinating coverage of special events. It was here that she met her first husband and here that she established her television career.

Ingrid and Chris were soon dating. 'Our first date was at an Indian restaurant,' said Ingrid. 'There was lots of talking, we both have quite a lot to say for ourselves.' And Tarrant was open with his new girlfriend about his turbulent life – which ended pretty much the moment he met Ingrid. 'We had lots of laughs, but marriage certainly wasn't on our minds,' she said. 'Chris told me he'd been through a wild patch. I always trusted him completely – and I was amazed that he was prepared to take on someone with two young babies.'

And so began the renaissance of Chris Tarrant, family man. By his own admission, Tarrant had not really enjoyed his wild days and soon found he was much happier in a settled relationship with Ingrid – and the mutual attraction did nothing to hurt matters. Both admitted that they spent as much time in bed as they could in those early days and that compatibility soon surfaced in day-to-day matters too.

Ingrid is the perfect woman for Tarrant. As vital, funny and lively as him, she is one of the few people who can actually out-talk him and who can hold her own with him in the room. And to this day, the affection between them is obvious: they will give each other bear hugs and sometimes appear like teenagers out on a date rather than a couple in their 50s who have been together for 20 years.

And it's not overstating it to say that Ingrid saved him. Tarrant himself once said, 'Ingrid changed me and made me feel there was a point to staying with one person again.' She came just in time too. On the one hand she gave him an alternative to a lifestyle that could have ended with Tarrant as a seedy drunk, while on the other she was there during the difficult years as far as his television career was concerned. For no matter how bad things got, Chris now had someone to go home to.

It soon turned out that it was a classic case of opposites attracting. In recent years, Tarrant was asked how he and Ingrid would manage if they went on *Millionaire* as contestants together. 'We would disagree on every question,' he announced. 'We argue all the time about everything and anything and we always have. She's a city girl, I'm a country bum. She's very tidy, I'm very untidy. It's extraordinary that we ever got together, but I love her to bits. I would be the one saying, "I'm not risking it," and she would insist we gamble. I do enjoy sitting there with my wooden spoon stirring it when the couples argue.'

And if some of the women Chris has worked with are to be believed, he was very lucky to find her. The English male is notoriously bad at getting on with the English female – perhaps Ingrid's Norwegian background helped here – and, with his public-school background, Chris had not grown up with women and so didn't always know how to treat them. It wasn't his fault – millions of Englishmen have exactly the same problem. But it did mean that not every woman succumbed to his charms. 'He is rather clumsy and schoolboyish,' complained one of his female colleagues. 'Not to mention patronising and chauvinistic.' It didn't matter. He loved Ingrid and Ingrid loved him, whatever his supposed faults.

And now, with his domestic life back on track, Chris got another big break. In 1984, five years after he'd left *Tiswas*, and five years spent with no really outstanding success, a call came out of the blue. Would Chris be interested in acting as a DJ on the station? You bet Chris would. In fact, it was to put him on top again, eventually leading him to become Britain's most highly paid television presenter. But at the time it took everyone by surprise. The standard career move was to move from radio to television – not vice versa. Chris, however, didn't care. He'd been given a chance to make it to the big time again and he seized it with both hands.

'Most people do radio for years, hoping that one day they will be on television,' he said. 'I've done it the other way round. I discovered radio in my mid-30s and think it's wonderful. It's so instant, I think Aspel and Wogan were at their best on the radio. I'm terribly critical of myself. I

79

rarely watch myself on television. I think I cock up a lot of things. The good thing about radio is that I can talk myself out of trouble.'

It couldn't have come at a better time and Tarrant knew it. 'Along came Capital Radio in 1984,' he said. 'I was plugging a book of silly anecdotes and doing the rounds of various radio stations. The controller of Capital heard me telling my stupid stories and rang my manager. So I made my first foray into radio doing a Sunday lunchtime show. It was given the daft title *Lunday Sunchtime*. I just used to be silly. I was also working at *TV-am*, where I met Ingrid. I did the Capital show for a summer and thought that would be it. Then I was asked to do a daily lunchtime show.

'I lived in Warwickshire but Paul Vaughan, my manager said, "You'd be mad not to sign this contract – it's fantastic." So I did and it was brilliant. I had freedom to do as much TV as I wanted. My show finished at 1pm and I could be back at my pub in Warwickshire for last afternoon orders. It was a fantastic life. I had a big house in the country with badgers round my door. Then I signed a one-year contract in 1987 for the *Breakfast Show* and I've been there ever since.' And working alongside him for many years, until they were to have a protracted and spectacular fall-out, was the weather girl Kara Noble, alongside Russ Kane, who reported on traffic from the Flying Eye.

Doing the morning show alone without the rest of his work would be gruelling for a lot of people, but Tarrant is equipped with a great deal of stamina. He has never found the early morning starts a problem – possibly as a result of all those early morning fishing expeditions – and has not had to alter his lifestyle one jot for the show. 'The night before I did the first show in 1987, I went to bed at 8.30 like a good boy, lay their like a prat for a couple of hours and then went over to the pub,' he recalled. 'I just don't need that much sleep. Now I've got the early morning stuff down to a fine art. A nice man from Capital rings me at 5.45 in the morning and says, "Are you up?" I have a bath and all that and it takes me 20 minutes to get in from Esher at that time in the morning. Funny thing is that I have no concept of a rush hour. I sit there listening to reports about hold-ups on the Robin Hood roundabout every morning, but I've never seen one.'

As it happened, the radio suited Chris's breezy persona down to the ground. It still surprises people that he has a public-school and university education, because his blokeish everyman persona makes him popular with all social types. But he fitted into Capital immediately, soon becoming known as Chrissy-wissy, and it was there that he made the acquaintance of one Sophie Rhys-Jones who was doing PR for the station, a friendship that was to cause quite a furore in the years to come.

And so Tarrant transferred the 'zoo' format to radio (another innovation that took place some years before Chris Evans came along). It worked just as well on the airwaves as it had done on television and it was wildly popular with the listeners.

'Hi,' a typical introduction would begin, 'today we have the bank robber who used a cucumber instead of a gun.' Music would play. 'What are you lot about?' Chris would continue. 'Do you know how many of you called up on April 1? Yes, April 1. To speak to our mantra line. Mantra line. April 1. Fourteen. Yes, fourteen thousand.' There would be more music and then a jingle. 'Chris Tarrant. A legend in his own trousers.' It's not difficult to see why it went down so well: it is exactly the sort of undemanding and yet fairly amusing banter that takes the edge off the early morning.

Chris claimed not to find it an effort. 'I'm quite natural,' he said to one interviewer. 'This could be me talking to you on Line 3 on the radio this morning. I don't know you from Adam, but it's like, "Hello, mystery caller." I don't find it remotely difficult to be on the radio wittering, live, every morning of my life.'

And so, as Chris began to flourish on Capital, he was able to keep a toe in televisual waters with his string of unmemorable game shows. It was an ideal counterpoint: his frustration at not being able to come up with another big television hit was offset by his growing popularity as a DJ. His personal life was flourishing too. Chris bought his home in Esher and, four years after they started dating, Ingrid and her children moved in when in 1989 she found she was pregnant. In October, she gave birth to the first of their two children together, Samantha. The couple were delirious but, at that time, both were still set against marriage. 'I'm very happy, but I don't want to marry again,' said Chris. The scars from his time with Sheila still ran deep – but he was showing signs of wanting some sort of permanent commitment. 'When I got pregnant with our first child, Chris suggested that I changed my surname to Tarrant by deed poll to keep the family uniform,' said Ingrid.

Chris still appreciated other women, but no longer wanted to sleep with them. He also admitted in finding them unfathomable. 'I find women really attractive,' he said. 'Always have done. Still do. I am definitely a man's bloke. I don't really have many one-to-one friendships with women. They are completely incomprehensible. When you are young, you are expecting to find the ideal partner for the rest of your life. Nonsense. You get older. You compromise.' Chris Tarrant had clearly grown up.

He also treated Ingrid very differently from Sheila. He still worked incredibly long days and then made time for his fishing, but he was beginning to realise that relationships need to be worked at. Asked what the most romantic thing he had ever done was, Chris replied, 'I once took my then girlfriend, now wife, to Paris for lunch on Valentine's Day.' He might not have understood women – but he was clearly beginning to understand what they liked.

And he was winning over listeners to Capital in their droves. Although often asserting that he doesn't succumb to self-doubt, Chris was proving a dab hand at self-deprecation. One of the jingles at Capital ran, 'Chris Tarrant, a legend in his own trousers. Dashing. Debonair. Dickhead.' Early morning listeners to commercial music radio stations do not want to have to digest philosophy with their cornflakes and Tarrant, while knowing rather more about philosophy than many of his listeners realised, was happy to oblige.

Jokes, of course, made up a huge part of the package, alongside the music and quirky news. But there was something else as well – something that perhaps explained events that were to happen years later. Right from the start, Kara Noble was the subject of Chris's jokes and some of them could be cruel. He would regularly introduce her as 'Kara, the weather girl with knees larger than her breasts'. Kara would take it in good part, of course, but Tarrant might have overestimated her. With a fine line in self-deprecation, he might genuinely have believed that Kara didn't mind the jokes. He was to be proved wrong.

The secret of it was that Chris – unlike some other morning DJs – knew his audience and knew exactly what they wanted. 'People who listen in to breakfast shows are delicate and vulnerable,' he said, 'and, once they find a programme they like, they want everything about it to stay exactly the same. People are listening to me wittering on while they are having a bath, chasing their kids, having sex, coping with a hangover or rush-hour traffic. I sometimes wish I could be a fly on the wall in a dozen different homes.' He did, however, rein in when serious world events happened. 'Being sombre isn't what people expect when they tune into me in the morning,' he said. 'On the other hand, I don't want to sound like a heartless idiot.'

Tarrant has often been accused of arrogance and there's no doubt that he can have a high-handed manner. But that accusation misses the point. Tarrant says he doesn't suffer from self-doubt because he doesn't, not in order to rile his nervy fellow presenters. And those years in the wilderness made him appreciate quite how lucky he was. Asked how he managed that early morning liveliness, he confessed, 'To be honest, some mornings I don't know myself.

'I can arrive feeling absolutely dreadful, but by 6.35am I think that life isn't that bad and a smile creeps into my voice and by 7am I'm feeling good. I have been bloody lucky, really, I don't have an enormous talent. I'm just larger than life. All I know is what you see and hear is an extension of me. I am professionally happiest when I am being myself. But I'm not larger than life at home. You couldn't stand living with me if I was like my radio show 24 hours a day.'

And the radio show was proving so popular elsewhere that in 1990 Radio 1 attempted to lure Tarrant on board. Radio 1 is seen as the Holy Grail in some quarters where the breakfast slot is concerned, but Tarrant turned it down. 'I mean, there's no need for a national station like Radio 1, is there?' he said. 'When I hear Radio 1 telling me about a traffic jam in Falmouth I think, what's that got to do with me? London is the best place to work: there's an extraordinary range of people who listen to me. It's not just the "Jack the lads" in Bethnal Green waking up with their girlfriends; there are a lot of ABC1s out there. The show has a weekly audience of 25 million.'

It was not only the locality of the show – Tarrant had a particular knack of lighting upon topics that were important to the man on the street. On one occasion, he complained furiously about faulty cashpoints, raging, 'Twice this week I've failed to get cash at 5.30am in central London. I've also had to go without cash for two weekends because I can't find a machine with money in it. The machine says, "Please try later." I can state loud and clear that the service does not work for me. For the last two weekends, every machine I tried had run out.'

A bad-tempered rant by a man who had the airtime to do it, you might have thought – but the Capital switchboard was promptly swamped with listeners desperate to tell how they, too, had had bad experiences of cashpoints. For that is the point with Chris. The listeners feel that he is talking to each one individually and they want to respond. 'I couldn't believe the number of people who said they've had similar experiences,' said Tarrant, who was clearly taken aback. 'I've had a letter from my bank manager telling me they are reviewing the system. I can't wait.'

And he certainly had enough cash in that bank account. He raised a few hackles by joking that he was now booked until the end of 1991 and, 'I have tried to cut it down by raising my fees, but all that did was get me more work and more cash! I don't care who I work for, as long as they pay me lots of money! I am a freelance operator and I am available to the highest bidder.' In other words: rivals – watch out.

But, he insisted, money was not the motivation. 'I am very well-off now, there is no point in denying it,' he said. 'But money is not a driving force. I love my job and leave my agent and his mafia to extract as much money as they can for me. I keep an eye on finances and do most things I am offered.' And this statement should not be viewed with too cynical an eye. Of course Tarrant liked the money – who wouldn't? – but the fact that he was earning so much was also the proof of his success. If you are the highest-paid entertainer around, the reasoning goes, then you are also the best. Chris has often spoken of enjoying the competition with rival DJs – and why shouldn't he? After all, he's always won.

But despite his newfound success and happiness with Ingrid, the couple were still no nearer marrying. In fact, Tarrant was still pretty negative about the whole idea. 'Neither of us has much faith left in marriage as an institution,' he said. 'We have both been divorced and it is painful. We have been together a couple of years and we are very happy. I feel that any slight change – like marriage – might spoil it. It may sound like a typical male cop-out, but neither of us is in any hurry to try it again. I would definitely advise my kids to think very carefully before getting married. In my day, a lot of couples went down the aisle without giving it much thought. But I don't think today's youngsters need much advice. They seem totally aware of the dangers. If their parents are not divorced, then they will know someone at school whose parents are.' It was, happily, a point of view that was to change.

Tarrant was very savvy in another way too – he has always refused to endorse any political party. The casual observer might surmise that he is almost certainly a Conservative – he's not averse to grumbling abut tax, amidst much else – but he's never come out and said so. In fact, he professes to hate all politicians. This is a wise move. If he came out in support of one party, supporters of the other might turn against him, and he wasn't risking that. Instead, he remained Chris Tarrant, Everyman, a much wiser move. 'I have been asked to do ads for most of the parties, but I avoid things like that,' he once said. 'I don't have very strong opinions anyway [sic]. Kenny Everett and Ben Elton stand on platforms with politicians, but that is not for me.'

What was also not for him, at least not at the rate he had been doing them, was voice-overs. In the lean days these had been a godsend but, given that he was now earning money hand over fist, Tarrant didn't need the money so much, and so he cut back on them. It was estimated that Chris had been doing an incredible 35 voice-overs every month – and this on top of his radio and television work. (Although, if he got paid £5,000 a shot, that was an additional £175,000 a month that he was earning, so you could see the appeal.) But, even for the hardest-working man in showbiz, something had to give.

'It was ruining my life,' said Tarrant. 'Having got up at six in the morning to do a breakfast show, I'd get home in the afternoon and then the phone would ring and I'd have to go back into London to record a voice. There came a point when I thought it wasn't worth it. It was ruining my lifestyle, my sleep pattern, my family life and everything else. There's no use pretending why I do so many, I can't say it's for my RSC training. But the money I have earned from it probably paid for my mansion in Surrey and my Mercedes – so I don't knock it.'

But Tarrant's sleep pattern is not that of other men. And in truth, he did himself no favours by repeatedly pointing out that not only was his radio show massively successful, but that he did the whole thing on practically no sleep. He did one interview after a programme that had followed a marathon fishing session, and mentioned that he hoped the listeners detected no sign of fatigue. 'Although I did mention on air that I had come to the studio from an all-night fishing session, I don't think anyone will have noticed that I'm tired,' he said brightly.

'I did think, when I left the other blokes fishing on the bank at 5.30 [am], that I might have difficulty, but it was OK,' he said. 'Got here at 6.30, bluffed my way through the start of the show, put on a record, bluffed my way through to the traffic spot and everything was fine. The great beauty of radio is that you can hide. No one is going to say, "Good God, look at Tarrant today, has he been up all night?" or even, "What is Tarrant wearing today?" We've just heard that we've won the Gold Medal at the International Radio Festival in New York. Apparently this means that we are now the best in the universe.' It was all good, bumptious stuff – and guaranteed to make at least some hackles rise.

But it was also true. By the early 1990s, half of Greater London was now tuning into Chris's show on Capital – a feat that his young rival, Chris Evans, has never managed to achieve. Tarrant was now possibly the most successful DJ ever, and Capital was possibly the most successful local radio station in the world. Kara and Russ had by now become celebrities in their own right, while sitting on top of the world and looking down was Chris. And he was constantly rubbing everyone's noses in it too. How was he so cheerful all the time? he was asked. 'Because they pay me a fucking fortune!'

But there was still a very different side to Tarrant and one which not many people saw. He was getting better than ever at separating the personal and the professional and such was his wacky public persona that not many people realised there was a quieter person underneath. Kara Noble did, though.

'There is this terribly soft side to Chris,' she said. 'He told me once that every morning before he leaves home at 5am, he sneaks into his youngest daughter Sam's bedroom to look at her sleeping. He said it keeps him sane. But then ten minutes later, when we're on air, he's abusing me and telling everyone I've got a huge bum and a wart on my nose. He once said, "Over to Kara the weather girl who has knees bigger than her breasts." When I first encountered him on a test run-through, I thought I would burst into tears. But now I know it works on radio and that there is this other side of Chris.' That's as maybe, but that jibe had clearly registered. Trouble was building up ahead.

Chris's children also had to learn to deal with the two different sides of their father. On air he was zany; off air he was strict. It was a balance everyone had to strike. 'Although, obviously, I am a larger-than-life dad, I don't want them to think that it's any big deal,' he said. 'It's just a job that I do and I don't want people boring them in the playground because of it. I think they are very balanced about it, they tend not to take too much notice of it. It's like it's another me. I hope they are generally proud of me, but no more than any child would be of their father. Jen doesn't like Tarrant. She says, "That's not you, that's you at work. I like you when you're real. When you're just Dad."

And, of course, the cheesy television shows were still continuing in the background. Yet another forgettable offering cropped up: *Crazy Comparisons*, an afternoon show in which celebrities attempted to guess the identity of mystery stars. *The Ascent Of Man* it wasn't, but it kept the bucks flowing in. He needed them too. One of the ways that Tarrant chooses to relax is by going on long, exotic holidays, such as a fishing expedition to Alaska. 'They say, after two weeks there, the Eskimo women become peculiarly attractive,' he joked. 'But then so do the polar bears.' Other nondescript offerings included *Hotline, Blimp Over Britain* and the *6 O'Clock Show*. The critics carped but Tarrant didn't care – he was laughing all the way to the bank.

And it was almost as if he was determined to prove that there was nothing he couldn't do. In 1992, Tarrant managed another first: he broadcast two breakfast shows in one day – one in London and one in New York. It was an extraordinary feat. He left his home as usual at 5am, and was broadcasting as usual shortly afterwards. Then, 'At 9.49 I was running down the corridors talking into a microphone. I jumped on the back of a motorcycle to a King's Cross helipad and I was flying past Big Ben at 9.53.' He flew to Heathrow, where he boarded Concorde and arrived in New York three hours later.

'Phew, we made it,' said Chris brightly as he settled into the studio – and began to broadcast his second show of the day.

The early 1990s were not an easy time for local radio stations because of the dip in advertising revenues and, indeed, Capital did not emerge unscathed. But it didn't fare anything like as badly as its competitors: in 1992, at the height of the recession, turnover was almost unchanged at £32.3 million. And a good deal of that came from the 'master of burble, bunkum and baloney' – Mr T. It's no wonder Capital pays him so much – his show was responsible for keeping so much of London tuned in and keeping the station's turnover so solid. Chris Tarrant, superstar DJ, was clearly on the up.

6

TARRANT RETURNS TO TV

Not, of course, that he'd ever been off it. But, as his personal life grew increasingly happy and his career at Capital flourished, he finally began to make the kind of programmes that were shown in the evening, rather than the afternoon, and that he could actually be proud of – to an extent, at any rate. But then that is the way that life goes. When he was desperately in need of a little luck in the early 1980s, little came Tarrant's way. When, however, his life had picked up and he didn't need further triumphs, he got them anyway. But then, of course, nothing succeeds like success.

Alongside his radio show, Tarrant was now being signed up for two new television shows: *The Main Event* and *Tarrant On TV*, which started its run on January 20, 1990. The latter was to become a long-running series of gloating over nonsensical television clips from different countries, and pretty much took up entirely where Clive James had left off. Again, it suited Tarrant's personality – affable, blokeish and just one of the lads. 'I'm just a silly, irreverent person,' said Chris, as he signed a few more lucrative contracts. 'I don't want to be taken seriously. I want to carry on doing what I do.'

He was able to carry on doing what he did but, within the industry at least, he was being taken very seriously indeed. A professional from the top of his flaxen head to the tip of his (then) ill-shod toes, Tarrant displayed absolutely no signs of prima donna-like behaviour: he got on and he did the job. 'He's sharp, great to work with and always on "receive",' said Danny Greenstone of Grundy TV, producer of *The Main Event*. Nicholas Barrett, producer of *Tarrant On TV*, agreed. 'Most of all, he's funny and has the ability to say things other people are thinking,' he said.

Tarrant On TV was by no means popular with everyone. 'The successful way of getting gratuitous filth on to the television these days is to have programmes about other programmes, principally foreign,' snapped one critic, before criticising the show for lingering over the naked body of a blonde woman, a shot Tarrant dismissed with the words, 'That's Finnish television for you.' But, given the complete lack of complaints to the switchboard, it was clear not everyone took so dainty a view.

Indeed, it soon began to gain popularity. The second show centred on American television and, despite more complaints from the critics that it was turning into some sort of a freak show, audiences were tuning in. LWT had been cautious and initially only gave Tarrant a six-programme trial, but it quickly became obvious that the format worked. It certainly gave an insight into other cultures – even if the insight wasn't always what the viewer was expecting.

'Iron Curtain TV used to be very restricted,' said Tarrant. 'But since Glasnost, the floodgates have opened and the most extraordinary stuff is coming out. Most countries seem to have a Benny Hill lookalike doing the same sort of stuff – only a lot ruder.' Nor was it just the Eastern Europeans who plumbed new depths of vulgarity. The programme featured one Spanish chat show in which everyone, the host, guests and audience, appeared in the nude. 'There are a lot of bosoms on display but no dangly bits,' said Tarrant. 'It's very funny – Aspel should try it. A lot of Euro humour is the sort of stuff we were laughing at 20 years ago. But I wouldn't say our television is tame – we've just grown up a bit.'

So much for European sophistication, but who cared? The audience certainly didn't and Tarrant began to ride high again. And, finally, he and Ingrid tied the knot. Initially, Tarrant was 'very against remarrying. I was very wary, although the kids were very for it. Whenever we passed a wedding shop, one would say, "Daddy, wouldn't Mummy look lovely in that dress," and I'd leg it down the road. Then one day, I suddenly couldn't remember what my objections were. We already had the babies. We were already committed. Nothing was going to change. So why not? It has given all the children stability, a cornerstone. And Ingrid and I are good together. She is very quick tempered, whereas I'm a brooder. When things bug me, I go into my room and brood. I keep things to myself, perhaps too much.'

The proposal, when it finally arrived, was typical Tarrant. He had been drinking heavily and was high as a kite. 'We had been together for about seven years when Chris proposed,' Ingrid said. 'First of all, I didn't say yes or no. We were having such a great night I said to him, "You're so drunk I don't think you know what you're asking, let's just wait and see." The next day he said he had meant every word and even asked me again. On the big day I had to remind myself that my maiden name was already Tarrant because of that deed poll change.'

The ceremony took place in May 1991 at their local parish church in Cobham, Surrey. Ingrid was three months pregnant, although, given that they already had a daughter together, that was nothing to do with why they married, and once the decision was made, they acted fast. 'Ingrid and I decided to get married almost on the spur of the moment,' said Tarrant. 'It was a case of "Let's do it now or in six months when I am next free." We got a special licence and everything and luckily we didn't get too much press attention because we did it on Cup Final day. She is my best friend and we are expecting another addition in November. Don't ask me what I want – I'll come out with that cliché, "I don't mind as long as it's perfect." Of course, I wouldn't mind a boy, because I haven't got one of those of my own. Mind you, a carp would be nice.'

He got his wish. On October 30, 1991, Ingrid gave birth

to the couple's second child, Toby Charles. 'It is great, finally, to have a son to take fishing,' a jubilant Tarrant exclaimed. 'I'm always off on my own down at the river!' But he was making time for his family, as well as entertaining his elder daughters at the weekend. 'Chris's children from his first marriage to Sheila never lived with us – they have fled the nest now,' Ingrid explained. 'But, when they were younger, we used to have them here every weekend. We were very fortunate that they and the rest of the children got on and always had a good time together. Chris was and is very good like that; irrespective of work, every weekend was devoted to seeing his girls.'

And it turned out that they'd made the right decision by getting married at last. 'For years I'd said that I didn't want to know about marriage but, since we did the deed, in a funny way, things are better,' Chris said. 'I don't know why. I think it's mainly now that the kids feel very secure. They prefer it. Our wedding day was brilliant. Our honeymoon was 48 hours in the Claridges Hotel in London.' Two months later, the couple finally managed a slightly longer break.

Chris had always worked long hours but by the early 1990s, given his radio career, his television career, his family and his fishing, he was now regularly working 19-hour days. Tarrant is blessed with the kind of constitution that can tick over on four hours' sleep a night, which is just as well given that he has to get up at 5am, but now started an annual lament: just how much longer could he carry on?

'Sometimes I wonder how long I can go on,' he said in an

interview in 1991. 'Luckily, although I don't look after myself, I have an amazing constitution and am as strong as a horse. I gave up smoking 60 cigarettes a day, but I now smoke about 12 cigars a day, which I must do something about. I've tried going to a gym, but I hated it. I jogged for a week last year, but it made me feel bloody awful. My dietary habits are hopeless too. I have long blasts of not eating anything at all and then shove a great slab of something into my tummy. I often feel like a drink at 10.30am. I sometimes think, This is the beginning of the end – Betty Ford clinic here I come! But I console myself, saying that, by anyone else's time, it is at least 1.30pm.'

This uncharacteristic self-doubt did not last long. Some canny souls have observed that Tarrant tends to ponder giving up his job once a year and that once a year tends to coincide with renegotiations for his contract and, certainly, he bounces back almost immediately. It's not that surprising that colleagues sometimes complain about his perceived arrogance, given the way he talks about his job, but that's just Tarrant.

He may boast a little, subconsciously or not, but he's never behaved like the likes of Chris Evans. No matter how bad the previous night's drinking binge he is always in the studio on time, he doesn't humiliate his colleagues on air and he doesn't drone on about buying his own radio station. He doesn't mention the worth of his house and how much he gets paid. He just talks abut the fact that he can do the job.

And he was being well paid for it too. By the end of 1991

those early morning starts may have seemed a touch more palatable due to the fact that his contract with Capital was now bringing him £300,000 a year. And with all the other work he was doing, including those television shows and his voice-overs, he was now earning about £1 million in total, which was not bad for someone who had been written off only a couple of years earlier as a has-been. It also made him Britain's highest-earning television star and he was not foolish with his money – he began investing in the stock market, building up a fortune that is now worth at least £20 million.

Chris has always denied that he does all the work on offer, pointing out that weekends are sacrosanct and are to be spent fishing or with the family. But Kara Noble saw it at firsthand from the outside. 'It's like he can't say no,' she said. 'Sometimes he can appear quite hard. He is very disciplined and he certainly doesn't suffer fools gladly.' It is from this excessive workload that Chris got a reputation for being fond of money – or concerned that one day it would dry up, just as it had threatened to after *Tiswas* – but as long as he could cope with it, why not?

Nor were his interests now solely confined to radio and television. In the early 1990s, the famously unkempt Tarrant got involved in, of all things, menswear. He teamed up with the Italian designer Dino Gemma to set up a menswear chain, Made In Italy. As with so much else, it all happened by chance. Gemma saw Tarrant on television, rang him up and 'told him he looked like a bag of shit', said Gemma. The two met some weeks later at a party and Gemma offered to make

Tarrant an Italian suit for free. They kept in touch and a year later, when Gemma decided he was going to set up a business, Chris asked if he could come in too.

'At the time I was doing another series of *Tarrant On TV* and was wandering around the suit shops in London with LWT's seemingly bottomless chequebook to buy outfits for the show,' Tarrant revealed. 'Even though I was spending someone else's money, I thought it was outrageous to be spending £800 for a jacket just because it's Italian. Dino said he wanted to start a company selling Italian men's clothes at reasonable prices. That struck a chord with me and we decided to go into business together.'

It immediately turned out that the two worked well together. Each put up £150,000 and leased a site in west Croydon: Made in Italy was born. They cut costs by getting involved in production and cutting back on profit margins, managed to sell the clothing at about 60 per cent cheaper than it was elsewhere and found they had such a success on their hands that they were able to open two more branches, in Woking and Romford. Gemma did the hands-on work, choosing the stock and setting prices, while Tarrant involved himself in strategy and expansion.

'Basically, Dino would like to be able to open ten shops because he loves the business so much,' said Tarrant. 'So my role is to tell him to calm down and take it easy. I'd like to expand, as long as I don't have to wake up at 3am and worry about what's happening in Tunbridge Wells.

'I get a very different buzz about this to doing radio and

TV work. We had a birthday party here last week and decided not to sell any suits because it would be an insult to try and take money off our customers. After about half an hour of sitting around eating peanuts and drinking wine, I thought, sod it and opened up the tills. I managed to flog loads of suits to some Irish bloke I'd never met. The big difference is that, in everything I've ever done before, I've never actually seen the money I make. All I get is a piece of paper from my agent telling me what I earned and what he earned and a bank statement. When I spend the money, I use a credit card. With the shops, I can see the cash pouring into the tills. That's such a great feeling.'

Whatever he may say, Tarrant is clearly a man who likes money and he didn't treat this as a vanity company, as so many other celebrities are prone to do. High-profile restaurants owned by actors who never actually go to them are commonplace on 'Planet Celebrity'; a solid business venture that does not depend on the identity of its owners is not. 'A lot of showbiz names buy a restaurant or a disco in the middle of nowhere and expect it to make money,' he said. 'They get out there once every two years and the venture always collapses, often with the manager doing a runner with the proceeds. I'm not interested in playing at being a businessman – this is the real thing.' And it has been noticeable that, ever since then, he has actually been better dressed.

Tarrant the Tyrant had become Tarrant the Tycoon and now television work was really pouring in. He was chosen to introduce the new week-day channel Carlton, which started up in 1993, and which was introduced to the world just after the New Year struck. Two minutes after midnight, Tarrant was on our screens. 'A star-studded 90-minute extravaganza with a host of guests' was promised, and Tarrant listed them all. 'The Chippendales, doing whatever it is they do with baby oil,' he proclaimed. Also up were stage hypnotist Paul McKenna, a Canadian comedian called Marty Putz and Paul McCartney, amongst various others. The usual frolics ensued: Chris turned up at St Thomas's hospital with a camera crew in tow to interview four women in labour and encourage their babies to appear; perhaps sensing that they'd be seeing enough of Tarrant anyway in later years, the babies stayed *in situ*. There was singing from the Inspirational Choir, an interview with McCartney and a great deal else. The critics hated it, the audience lapped it up and everyone carried on as normal.

The iffy shows had by no means disappeared from our screens. As a sort of prequel to what would become his most famous show, Tarrant took on a new programme called *Lose A Million*, with Honor Blackman doing the voice-overs. The idea was that the contestants had to lose a fictional £1 million in order to win £5,000 and they did this by getting the questions wrong. It was too trite to merit going into the details of the game: suffice it to say that the set was an unconvincing mock-up of a 1920s cruise liner and the catchphrase for the show was: 'Let's linger no longer, let's go lose some wonga'. Mercifully, it didn't last that long.

Even so, Tarrant's schedule got heavier than ever. How did

he keep going? 'Drugs,' said Tarrant with a straight face in an interview in 1994. 'That's how I do it. Write that down. Nah, it's not drugs. I went over to the States and I was sort of guest of the day on all these stations. Christ, but the amount of coke they do. It's really worrying. What a way to go, eh? Look what I get. Sugar-free mints. When I started this, Noel Edmonds said to me that nobody could do a breakfast show for more than a year, two years maximum. But I've been here since 1987 and it's fine. I still get the buzz.'

And Chris was increasingly becoming a family man. He was now presiding over a family of six: his two elder daughters, who he endeavoured to see as much as possible, Ingrid's two children and Samantha and Toby. In all, he was appearing increasingly thoughtful. The breezy persona went from strength to strength on the radio, but at home Chris had his priorities sorted. 'I make time for things,' he said. 'I have to fish, I have to see my kids and I have to see my lady. I try not to work weekends and I take exotic holidays.'

While it is true that Chris's time in the wilderness made him all the more ambitious, it is equally the case that it made him more mature. In the days of *Tiswas*, he ruined his family life for his career, only to have that very career peter out shortly afterwards. And deep down, he knew it could happen again, no matter how much he fought to keep it. And so Tarrant really did begin to realise the importance of his family life: a solid base in a shifting world. He was bringing up Ingrid's children as his own and was well aware of his responsibilities.

'It's been hard for me and difficult for the kids too,' he

admitted. 'But, after five years, they are used to me, and have learned there are no different rules in the house for anybody. I see my own kids most weekends. Sometimes during the week I have a desperate need to see them and will drive 140 miles just to be with them for an hour. It sounds daft, but it makes me feel much better.'

And this change all came down to Ingrid. As in all the best relationships, theirs had deepened over time. Still clearly besotted with her, Tarrant was forever calling her 'very kind', 'incredibly sexy' and 'easily my best friend in the whole world'.

And, while many people would consider 19-hour days a pretty heavy workload, Tarrant was adamant that he'd got the balance right. It was Ingrid who showed him that 'family is actually far more important than work, and that you have to make time for it', he said. 'There is this myth about me, that I'll accept anything going. The phone rings and I'll say, "Yeah, yeah, I'd love to do that," whatever it happens to be. But it's not true. I've turned down bloody loads of work because it intrudes on my family time.'

The house in Cobham was a retreat. 'I need a nest,' Tarrant explained. 'We had the builders in for six months to create a house where I can hide. We keep the kids in the play room, keep the lounge for ourselves and I have an enormous study with stuffed fish and books where I can light a fire and look out at the river. I bought the house because there was a river at the end of the garden, but there are not many fish in it. I organised a fence near the river and screamed at the kids to be careful, but I'm the only one who has fallen in.'

As Tarrant's life became increasingly hectic, his desire to fish turned into an almost physical need and, despite – or perhaps because of – the hours he worked, he was still managing to fish about three times a week. 'I fish even if I only have a couple of hours to spare,' he said. 'I'll go at night, or in the summer at 3am and arrive at work afterwards feeling marvellous. It makes me feel I have done something with my day, not just earned money and paid bills. I have so much work tied up that sometimes I feel trapped. I enjoy the ride on the roller coaster but sometimes I want to get off.'

He was, though, being increasingly well rewarded for his pains, although he was keen to point out, 'I have never been a show-off about money. I like a large house because I need one. I also need a fast car [still a Mercedes] because I travel on the motorways a lot at strange hours. But I am strict with my kids and have brought them up to know that they can't get whatever they want.'

And Tarrant was certainly prepared to fight his corner when he deemed it necessary. In the autumn of 1994, *Tarrant On TV* was pulled forward in the Saturday night schedules in order to run against the BBC's new hospital series *Casualty*. But the fact that Tarrant's show was to be screened earlier in the evening than its usual 10.30 slot on Sundays enraged the star, who claimed that the programme's content would have to change accordingly, and it would thus lose viewers.

'In a moment of madness the ITV network have decided to plonk a very successful adult show right in the middle of family viewing time,' he snapped. 'It is war between the channels on Saturday nights and ITV controller Marcus Plantain is keen to limit the damage caused by *Casualty*. It won't be Holby General 17 million–Tarrant 0 but I know I am on a hiding to nothing. I just hope viewers give my show a chance.'

It is a mark of Tarrant's savvy at that stage that he did not automatically assume that his presence on the show would attract viewers. Unlike poor old Chris Evans, Tarrant was not making the mistake of believing his own publicity. He had worked on television for so many years now, with such varying degrees of success, that he knew that he himself, like every other presenter, was a product who had to be marketed properly. His massive success on the radio did not guarantee massive success on television and, when he did find the right format, it had to appear in the right time and place. He knew very well that no one owed him the time of day, let alone a slot on prime-time television and, once that slot was within his grasp, he was going to fight like a tiger to keep it.

And the programme certainly did offend some sensibilities. The TV watchdogs gave him a slap on the wrist for showing a German having sex on the show (in an advertisement for ceiling panels). He also upset some people when laughing at a clip of a shot of a man so fat he could die – unsurprisingly the man in question was appearing on the *Jerry Springer* show – and following the shot with the comment, 'And the really good news is that he got to the hospital in time ... for lunch.'

In fact, Tarrant claims that it was due to clips like that one that the way was paved for Jerry Springer's UK success. '*Tarrant On TV* is ground breaking,' he announced in 2000. 'We broke the *Jerry Springer Show* three years ago. It became so memorable from our clips that the rights were bought over here and the rest is history. I met Jerry at the National TV Awards recently. I didn't know whether he'd be pleased or angry to see me. After all, when we first showed the fights it was to have a laugh. I was pleased when he thanked me for making the show famous here.'

His radio career attracted no such complaints. As Tarrant's popularity continued to soar, he became increasingly scathing about his rivals – and with some reason. By the mid-1990s, he was pulling in two and a half million listeners, streets ahead of everyone else. Chris was delighted, saying that the competition helped. 'It's so weak at the moment,' he purred. 'Radio 1? Emma Freud? At lunchtimes? Discussing fallopian tubes? They've lost the plot entirely, haven't they?'

One of the ways that Chris kept – and keeps – his schedules going is by taking long and exotic holidays. But by this time the listeners adored him so much, they didn't want him to go away for a second. 'I don't come round your house saying, "Oh, you're on holiday again, you bastard,"' he complained to one journalist. 'But I always get, "You're always on holiday." I get people writing to me saying, "Can you please tell me when your summer holiday is so I can arrange to be on holiday myself?"

'To be honest, radio should not be that important. It's ridiculous. People are more sensitive in the morning. They have to have this thing which is part of their lives. Their routine is: turn on the radio, have Tarrant's voice in my ear – even if I can't stand him, he's got to be there. Get in my car, slice of toast in my mouth, point my car towards London or whatever. People have to have this. People are so sort of delicate first thing in the bloody mornings. This is how people bloody are.'

Still, it was a small price to pay. Given a choice between television has-been and one of the most popular radio presenters in the country – and very well paid, at that – it would be an odd person to opt for the former. Chris knew it too. And he knew that the reason for his success was that he related to the listener in the manner that most presenters simply don't. He was often called irreverent, but that was because, according to Capital Radio boss Richard Parks, 'He's the man who says the things his listeners are thinking. Whether it's jokes about Michael Jackson or digs at Margaret Thatcher.'

Tarrant himself was aware of this empathy with the listener, although he, as much as anyone else, was at a loss to explain it. 'People relate to aspects of me that are very much like themselves,' he said. 'That probably is it, actually. I'm either a lot like them or a lot like they would like to be. I actually don't understand it. I've never analysed it. I'm grateful for it but I don't understand.' As for the irreverence: 'People say I'm irreverent,' he says, 'but I never say anything you wouldn't say to your mates. It's just that I say it on TV or on the radio. It's just saying the first thing that comes into your head. Or sometimes – the second.'

Rather endearingly, just like his fans, Tarrant admitted to having heroes too, starting with Robert de Niro. 'I'd have to stand there being an absolute prat with my grubby little bit of paper saying, "Please, Mr de Niro," then boringly tell him about all his films. Don't you think he's just such a great actor? I can be very boring about Robert de Niro. The other is Billy Connolly. You can't help but laugh, you want to go wee-wee but you daren't.'

The holidays continued apace. In 1993 alone, the Tarrants managed to fit in Venezuela, New York, Norway and Zambia. But again – Tarrant needed it. It was his way to escape. He could also afford it. By 1993, he was estimated to be earning £400,000 a year from his Capital salary alone, and that's before taking into account all his television work and his business. That was at least four times higher than his nearest rival, Simon Mayo on Radio 1.

In fact, Tarrant's salary was now talked about so widely that Richard Parks felt the need to make a statement in praise of his star. 'Chris is great value for money,' he said. 'I know some other stations have pursued him mercilessly. I never comment on the earnings of our DJs, but we pay people on performances. Chris deserves to be the highest-paid DJ in the country simply because of the great talent he displays every day on his show. He is the best broadcaster in Europe and we wouldn't want to lose him.

'Since he started Capital's breakfast show seven years ago, the audience figures have gone through the roof. He had crucified our rivals. He gets an average of more than three million listeners a day – at least twice as many as Simon Mayo in London. People in London love waking up to him because he makes them feel happy with his great sense of humour. He's got his finger on the pulse.'

It seemed that the only way was up. Tarrant was the most popular, best-paid DJ in the country, enjoyed success both on television and in his private life and now owned a successful business. What could possibly go wrong? Quite a lot, as it happens.

7

CHRISSY-WISSY WINS AGAIN

As Tarrant continued to broadcast to the nation over its morning cuppa, one element of the show became increasingly marked. It was tormenting Kara. His jibes really were close to the knuckle – a lesser woman would not have been able to take it at all, let alone for as long as Kara did. Here's a sample: 'She's not very bright, you know. In fact, if she had one more brain cell, she'd qualify for pond life. And if King Kong wanted his bottom back, she wouldn't have a face. She lives in a hovel in the red-light district of Crouch End, drives an old rust bucket and is desperate for a man. She's also paid a pittance and doesn't deserve any more because she's so thick.'

Of course, Chris laughed it all off as an act, but could there have been genuine malice there? Or was Tarrant, who frequently admitted that he couldn't understand women, simply not aware of how cruel it seemed? Or was it, as Tarrant insiders have suggested, simply that Chris is most rude to the people he really likes? With retrospect, it's certainly not hard to see how the tension between the two of them built up, but, back in the early 1990s, both claimed it was all sweetness and light. In one interview, Chris revealed that he got letters from the listeners telling him not to be so horrible, but 'I don't take the slightest notice. She deserves everything she gets. I mean, just look at her. What has she come as today? She's got her horse blanket on again.'

In the background, Kara patiently explained that it was not a horse blanket, but a very expensive designer coat. 'But what would he know about fashion?' she said, nodding at Chris. 'I was a bit worried [about the teasing] but I soon realised it was all an affectation really,' Kara went on. 'He's only really rude to people he likes. In the end, I became the butt of his jokes, but people are very sympathetic. I had a letter yesterday from a man who sent a certificate for Chris to sign saying from now on he must be nice to Kara.'

In fact, the two had become so chummy that they were now friends. 'Chris is all talk and no todger,' Kara continued. 'It's a great working relationship. I've been to his house a couple of times and love his wife Ingrid and the kids. He forgot my birthday on July 13 despite the fact that I had been dropping huge hints for days. I was quite hurt, actually, but when I got home I found he had sent a bunch of flowers and champagne. The next day I tried to thank him on air and he wouldn't let me. Every time I tried, he kept turning my mic off. Apparently wherever he went, people were ticking him off for forgetting my birthday. I think he really felt bad about it.'

Chris was equally effusive about his on-air chum. 'You couldn't do it day after day with someone you genuinely didn't like,' he said. 'It all sort of grew and grew. She started coming in to do bits of weather and we found ourselves naturally getting into this banter. I love having lots of people to talk to around the studio, otherwise it would just be me and that would be boring. She has a very horny voice. Of course, she's like that, you know – desperate for a man but who would have her? I like Kara because she answers back. Both she and Russ were lucky to have been at the right place at the right time and it all gelled together. There's a whole London sympathy vote for her. She gets a regular correspondence from weirdos.'

Of course, Chris had been pretty lucky to be in the right place at the right time himself, and it must have been a little grating for Kara that he didn't acknowledge this. But the two seemed happy enough in their sparring matches, and Tarrant even had a nickname for her, Kara B Cakemix. Unsurprisingly, it was salacious in its origin.

'The B is easy,' said Kara. 'I used to be married to a producer called Simon Booker in the 80s and Chris used to call me Old Mother B. The Cakemix bit is a bit rude, actually. A listener sent me this rather strange book about sexual fantasies and we were all reading them out loud and having a good laugh. I don't want to be too specific, but the "cakemix" involved a housewife doing the Hoovering in the nude, covered in cakemix. The neighbours' dog comes into it as well and that's all I'm prepared to say. It's certainly not my fantasy.' Poor Kara. Just how much was the woman supposed to take?

By the mid-1990s, with Tarrant's stock soaring higher than ever, Virgin Radio, at that point owned by Richard Branson, made a concerted effort to get Chris on board. The approach became widely known, much to the chagrin of Virgin breakfast DJs Russ and Jono, who were currently minding the slot. Tarrant turned it down. 'It's a slap in the face for Richard,' said a Virgin insider. 'He was desperate to get Chris. It would have been a big boost for the station. Chris brings in a lot of business for Capital.' He did indeed – and perhaps he was wise not to move. He and the station clearly suited one another and a move elsewhere might have ended up cramping his style.

And he was certainly prepared to take risks. In 1995, Tarrant actually made people believe it was the wrong day of the week. On April 1, a Saturday, he, Kara and Russ came into the studio to broadcast, instead of the normal Saturday breakfast DJ Paul Phrear. He fooled a massive number of listeners: fully 5,000 phoned the Capital switchboards thinking they had their dates wrong (the listeners, that is – not Capital), while 20 actually got up and went into work, thinking it was Friday.

One woman worked for an hour without her colleagues

turning up before realising there was something wrong, a second turned up to a meeting she had already attended the previous day and a taxi driver threatened to sue Tarrant because he'd missed a lucrative appointment. Indeed, it really was going almost too far, although Tarrant himself was unrepentant. 'I was amazed by how gullible people are first thing in the morning!' he crowed.

If truth be told, Tarrant was lucky to get away without being punched on the nose. But there is something about him that allows him to get away with activities that would get most people in trouble. For some reason, people are prepared to overlook it when he goes too far, just as they will excuse the activities of a naughty, but fundamentally loveable child.

And so Tarrant went on to remain king of the airwaves, ubiquitous television presenter, businessman, fisherman and just about anything else he could fit into his schedule. And he could do it partly because he had so many people working with him who valued him and who smoothed his path through life. But he was about to get a nasty surprise. Tarrant is so totally focused on his own career that he sometimes forgets that other people have their own lives to think about too. That included some of his closest professional allies – and one of them was about to scarper.

It came as a nasty shock. It was April 1995, just four days after the Saturday stunt, and Kara Noble suddenly announced that she was leaving. She was going to co-host a rival show on the newly formed Heart 106.2 FM for a reputed £100,000-a-year salary. Initially, everyone was very polite about each other. 'I'm sorry to see her go, she's done a great job,' said Chris.

But behind the scenes there was some anger at her move. Capital was gearing itself up to a serious rival: Chris Evans was about to join the breakfast show on Radio 1. The feeling was very much that all hands were needed on deck and this was no time for one of Capital's stars, albeit a minor one, to be jumping ship. 'We made her and she has walked out at a difficult time,' said one Capital insider.

And indeed, it took about two seconds for this to turn into a full-on battle. Tarrant refused to let Kara say goodbye to the listeners on air, nor had he congratulated her on the new job. In fact, he was even refusing to take her phone calls. 'I think he has been very selfish, rude and insensitive, especially as the listeners see it as the end of a marriage,' said Kara. 'I would have loved to come in and say goodbye properly, but my name has just been eradicated from the books and I don't exist any more. It is like a George Orwell situation.'

Matters immediately escalated further. Perhaps unsurprisingly, it turned out that Kara had resented Tarrant's jokes at her expense and become increasingly fed up of being on the receiving end of some pretty cruel humour. 'Our on-air marriage was a sham,' said Kara. 'There was a friendship, but it was very patriarchal. He ruled. Well, he rules Capital Radio, so I was part of his harem, really. I wasn't really a wife.

'He knew I haven't been happy at the station this year for various reasons, but he didn't step in when he knew I was upset. He left me to suffer. He should have been more thoughtful about my feelings. He has the power to do anything and he chose not to. He has never really done much to help me. He did hurt my feelings a lot of times, not necessarily with what he said on air, but afterwards. He never showed his emotions. He was very businesslike. I suppose it is easier for him to be cold.'

Poor Kara. She was beginning to sound more like an ex-girlfriend than an ex-colleague though their relationship had been always purely professional. Certainly once started, the list of grievances rolled out.

'He would sometimes say I had a fat bottom or something like that,' she said. 'The fact that I knew I didn't have a fat bottom made it not so bad. But I still used to feel dreadful about it because there would probably be people listening who might have a fat bottom. I thought that could be offensive. I was kept in my place. Sometimes I was allowed to have an opinion but, if he didn't like it, he wouldn't talk to me for the rest of the show. I hoped he would be pleased for me getting this new job, but he wasn't. I am not a traitor. I understand that Chris seems to think my name is mud and that I left him to undermine his success with a new station, which is absolute rubbish. How he can think that of me I just don't know. I have gone to a new station because I have got a better deal.'

If Kara really thought Tarrant would be pleased for her, she was either foolish or naïve. For, while she knew that he had a deeper, quieter side off air – witness those remarks about watching his sleeping daughter – she massively underestimated the ambitious side of his character. No matter how much he objects to being called a workaholic, Tarrant exists to broadcast, whether it be on the radio or television, and, having once before experienced failure, he was determined it would never happen again.

That easy-going persona is quite genuine, but what it does is hide a steely ambition that will knock aside anything in its way. Tarrant may be easy-going in some respects, but he is the first to talk about how much he has trounced his rivals and, in his view of his career, you were either with him or against him. Kara had left to join the opposition. Tarrant saw it as a personal slight.

But perhaps Tarrant should have tried just a little bit to cover over the rift. For, when Kara left, she took something with her that was very valuable, something that was to cause such a furore that it even affected the ruling Head of State. That something was a photograph of Chris Tarrant and Sophie Rhys-Jones.

As it turned out, Tarrant had nothing to worry about with regard to his new flame-haired competitor. And Tarrant was jubilant. While outwardly maintaining that devil-may-care attitude to the world, he was actually fiercely determined to hang on to his position as Britain's number-one DJ – as Kara Noble had just found out to her cost – and in the summer of 1995 he faced his fiercest threat to date: Chris Evans. At the time, Evans was on a roll. He was seen as the bright new hope of British broadcasting, able to switch his zany humour from radio to television and back again, a wildly irreverent gust of fresh air blowing away the leaves of pomposity – in other words, a younger version of Chris Tarrant.

And so, would the young pretender be able to snatch Tarrant's crown? No, he would not. Tarrant beat him hands down when audience figures were published in August 1995: he still had over two million London listeners tuning in every day, compared to just 900,000 people in the capital turning on Radio 1. In fact, Evans was actually third on the list of weekly listening figures for the London area, falling not only behind Capital but also Radio 4. So much for youth.

Radio 1 was quick to defend its bright young star. 'It is frustrating to hear about traffic jams outside Sheffield, when all you want to know about is Hyde Park Corner,' said a spokesman for the station. 'But Radio 1 is not a London station. What matters is that we are the number-one breakfast show across the country. Radio 1 is not involved in the battle for the airwaves in London.'

Tarrant, however, was and he was jubilant about the figures. 'It is total domination over a fragmenting marketplace,' he said. 'Other presenters come and go, but London listeners can be assured of the loyalty of Capital.' In other words, he counted them in, he counted them out ...

The station was doing well financially too. The following year, half-year profits were up 23 per cent to £15.6 million: not bad for a local radio station. Tarrant, meanwhile, continued to amuse, on one occasion being phoned up by a listener called Andrew Williams. Andrew's wife Clare was in hospital in labour, but the baby was refusing to come out: could Tarrant help? Chris got the couple to put the phone to Clare's stomach and tried to persuade the baby to make its entrance live on Capital Radio. The baby declined and finally made an appearance after the show. His parents called him Oliver.

At the end of 1995, with both his radio show and *Tarrant On TV* in full swing, Tarrant launched yet another new series. Again it was panned by the critics – with some justification – but again the audiences liked it. This time their taste was inexplicable because the show in question was *Man O Man*, first put forward as a saucy version of *Blind Date*. It made *Tarrant On TV* look like *University Challenge*. Originally a German show, the format was now turning up all over the world, including Australia and the United States. Indeed, Tarrant had already seen it when the proposal was put to him.

'Where did I see it first?' he said a few months after the show got under way. 'It was in Germany, about three years ago. There was this bar full of demented drunken German ladies screaming abuse at a load of scantily clad men who kept getting pushed into swimming pools and I thought, That's a very strange piece of entertainment. So when I'd been chewing the fat about various programme ideas with Grundy TV [makers of *Man O Man*] they gave me a tape and I put it on and thought, Oh, it's that one. Are we sure about this?'

The idea was that ten men would try to prove to hordes of

screaming women that they were unbelievably attractive by way of various competitions, contests, question-and-answer sessions and so on. As the show progressed, the men would be pushed into a swimming pool until there were only two left, at which point the two would strip. Tarrant himself would be surrounded by ten hostesses as he commented on the proceedings and he assured everyone that Ingrid didn't mind a bit. 'I thought she'd go ballistic, but she told me to go for it,' said Tarrant. 'It's a rough job, but someone's got to do it. She is normally very critical, but she's got a good feeling about this show.'

Ingrid was proved right. The viewers loved it. The sight of a lot of women racing around in a kind of Bacchanalian frenzy went down a hoot. The critics, however, loathed it and spent much time agonising about the terrible state of television today. 'You knew that inevitably there would be a lot of flak and a lot of people saying, "This is the lowest TV has ever sunk,"' said Tarrant defensively. 'I went to lots of meetings before I signed on the dotted line, because I really did want to keep the 6.30–7pm family audience. I saw the Norwegian version – and bear in mind that I'm married to a Norwegian – and it was absolute filth.'

The English version was more about drunken women having fun and Chris professed to be taken aback by their Amazonian behaviour. 'I think it is the most shocking thing I've done,' he announced solemnly. 'It comes down to which of the blokes the women in the audience would like to shag and, as far as I can see, there is no rhyme nor reason for the choices made. The women are extraordinarily vicious. They sit there thinking, Let's get the bastard! And why? Because he's too good-looking!'

All in all, it gave poor old Tarrant quite a shock to peer into the abyss that is a woman's psyche. 'There's something horribly twisted about women's brains that men can't understand,' he went on. 'They want to nail the poor devils to a cross. They ask terrible, no-win questions and become quite hysterical at the answers. They have preconceptions about men and condemn someone as a smarmy git just because of the way he says "Hello". I have never yet been able to spot a man who will win. Every time I think someone is an obvious choice, he disappears within minutes. It proves I haven't a clue what women like about men – and I think that goes for most males.

'The older I get, the less I understand women. I think the gap between the sexes is getting wider, not narrower. I don't believe in the "New Man". I think men are confused and don't have a clue abut what women want. We don't know what our role is. I watched the Australian final of the show with my wife and some of her girlfriends and the man I thought would be the winner went in minutes and a wimp won.'

But, bemused or not, Chris had nothing to worry about as far as the show was concerned. It was a success and he was also pleased to have managed to make it family friendly. 'I didn't want to do big willy jokes in front of a leering bunch of hooting women,' he said. 'It's much more of a challenge to

Chris as a schoolboy – already the cheeky look and the mop of blonde hair made him stand apart from the crowd.

Today Is Saturday, Wear A Smile! *Tiswas* – the show that brightened up every youngster's Saturday morning. (*Top*) Lenny Henry does his David Bellamy impression, and (*bottom*) an interview with the notorious Phantom Flan Flinger.

Top: King Chris gets the *Tiswas* treatment.

Bottom: The *Tiswas* team together: Chris, Sally James and Trevor East.

Top: Chris surrounded by a bevy of lovelies in *Man O Man*.

Bottom: Sharing a joke with Tony Slattery in *Saturday Stayback*.

Top left: Chris with Sheila, his former wife and mother of his two daughters on their marriage day.

Top right: Chris with his father Basil during the National TV Awards at the Royal Albert Hall.

Bottom: The family man: (*left to right*) daughters Jennifer and Fia, father Basil, mother-in-law Arda Dupre, wife Ingrid and daughters Sammy and Helen.

Top: Chris reacts to the news that he has won best quiz show at the National TV Awards, and is congratulated by his wife Ingrid.

Bottom left: Chris with his children at a star-studded London movie premiere.

Bottom right: Dexter Walsh, Chris's stepson.

Chris in the days when the hair was a little longer, and the jackets a little wackier…

Chris and Ingrid at Tony Hadley's birthday party.

do a family version. And I think we've succeeded. OK, we have sexy hostesses and scantily clad men. But the fellas are in their boxer shorts, not standing with their dangly bits hanging out.'

Tarrant professed himself to be highly amused at the questions the women came up with and one in particular: what do you think of women drivers? 'What a bastard thing to ask a bloke!' cried Chris. 'The moment a guy is asked a question like that, he's out of it. There's no right answer. I would sit in the middle of these poor bastards and think, What are they going to ask next?

'There are no scripted questions. This isn't *Blind Date*. It would be crap if you had them saying, "I'd be your tiger and I'd roar all night." We had to stop them thinking in that *Blind Date* speak. We also had to cut out any questions that weren't within the bounds of decency for 6.15 on a Saturday night. Nobody's going to say, "Number one, have you got a big dick?" You can forget all about that.'

Even so, it did attract extraordinary amounts of criticism. Angela Rippon, no less, called it puerile. One critic labelled it, 'extraordinarily banal'. Tarrant professed himself to be totally unworried by the fuss and, with all the work he had coming in, that was undoubtedly true. He'd been in the business so long now that a little sniping wasn't going to bother him. 'I've been in a lot worse crap over the years,' he told one interviewer. 'Did you see *Cluedo*? What a pile of ... *Man O Man* was worth all the criticism because I thought it was such a good crack to make. There's nothing on earth to compare with 300 completely rat-faced women howling for male blood. People like you kept saying, "What's the point of it?" But you missed the point, because there was no point at all. It was just a laugh. No, the flak didn't bother me.'

Nor did turning 50, sometimes a difficult time in a man's life, especially if he's on television most of the time. But that didn't bother Tarrant either. 'Do I look as if I give a shit?' he asked somewhat baldly. 'Am I supposed to be putting my feet up and doing foreign affairs? No, I don't think it matters any more. Rod Stewart's 53.'

It was around then that comparisons with Chris Evans boiled over once again. Tarrant had quite clearly won the battle for London listeners, but Evans was by now making the news because he'd formed his own company, Ginger Productions. It meant he had total control over his own output and he was ultimately able to buy Virgin Radio and, when he went on to sell the company, it made him a very rich man. Tarrant was plagued by suggestions that he should do something similar.

'People ask me this every year, but the truth is I haven't got the time,' he snapped. 'Sure, it would be nice to have complete control over your output, but frankly, I don't need the hassle of running a company, worrying about the finance and the staff. It's not my scene. I never had the slightest career plan in my life. I can take it or leave it. I know I'll always work. I don't really take life too seriously. If I think something will work, I'll give it a go and then it's up to the viewers. That was the secret of *Tiswas*. We just went down the pub, wrote it and did it. And I hate contracts. I just want to do a job until I get fed up with it, then not be in one morning.' It was fighting stuff and – more than that – it kept Capital Radio on its toes.

Back at the breakfast show, business continued as usual. At around the time that Tarrant's contract came up for annual renewal, Chris would indulge in a public bout of soul-searching about his future. Should he pack it all in for a quieter life? Should he hand the precious breakfast show to a younger man – and just hope that Capital could keep all those listeners? 'I want my life back,' he said in 1998. 'I would love to continue doing radio, but I am not sure I can continue doing the breakfast show.

'It does knock you about and all the guys like Noel Edmonds have always said you can only do it for four years. I would love to have great chunks of my diary free. I want to spend more time at home with the kids, spend more time travelling. Sooner or later Capital will have to bite this bullet.' It worked. Frantic Capital executives promptly threw themselves at the nearest chequebook and Tarrant wearily decided that, yes, perhaps he could manage another year after all.

Pausing only to pick up awards for the 'Best Top 40 Station' and 'Best Music Personality' at the prestigious New York Radio Festival, Tarrant proceeded to lay into the competition, especially you-know-who. 'The last time Radio 1 had a serious audience was with Simon Mayo,' he said. 'Whatever they claim about Evans is nonsense. Radio 1 is not doing well. The wacky zoo style where everyone shouts in the background – we did that in 1985. I think it sounds outdated.' Nor was he overly impressed with Virgin's Russ and Jono: 'They have done nothing despite all the money.' In other words – yah boo sucks to the lot of you.

Of course, Tarrant and Evans were rivals not just on the radio, but on television too. Chris adopted a lofty approach. It was as if Evans was too small to bother him. What's more, Tarrant was so far ahead of him that he could even afford to give him praise – where it was due. 'I love [*Don't Forget Your*] *Toothbrush*,' he said. 'I am not sure about him on the radio. I am not copping out. I really have not listened to him enough to have an opinion.'

Talk about damning with faint praise. It got better. 'I am not sure about [*TFI*] *Friday*,' Tarrant went on. 'Bear in mind a large percentage of that quite small audience on Friday at six is going to be young, very young, and watching because Oasis or Blur are on. I don't really want my kids turning on the telly at six and hearing people say "f***". I just don't like a lot of effing and blinding that early in the evening.' So there you have it. People only tuned in because of Oasis and Blur, not Evans, and not many of them were tuning in anyway – 'large percentage of that quite small audience' – and when Evans himself was on air, standards slipped. Tarrant had made his own point of view pretty clear.

Of course, one difference between Capital Radio and Radio 1 is that the latter is for a young audience and the former is for everyone. Much the same could be said of the difference between the two Chris's television shows. Evans was presenting himself as the anarchic face of youth which, by its very nature, has a short shelf life, whereas Tarrant was coming across as an affable everyman. Whether you were 8 or 80 Tarrant was broadcasting to you – hence the secret of his mass appeal and the reason he has outlasted so many breakfast show rivals.

But even he did sometimes overstep the mark. As another series of *Tarrant On TV* got up and running, network bosses decided that one potential offering was just beyond the pale and banned it from the show. It was, believe it or not, clips from the Swedish Enema Championships and showed full-on scenes of colonic irrigation. Tarrant accepted their decision. 'It goes way past the acceptable level on the British taste meter – but what we can show is still really funny.'

To everyone's surprise, giving the pasting it got, *Man O Man* was recommissioned for a second series. This time round, there would be 100 more women in the audience, it would be 15 minutes shorter and the hapless contestants' mothers would be on hand to give their verdict on their sons. Meanwhile, Melissa Messenger and Philippa Forrester would be on hand to join in the fun. Tarrant was jubilant.

'I nicknamed the last audience the hen party from hell and I've no doubt that it will be the same this time,' he said triumphantly. 'I had so much fun in the last series. It's remarkable how women behave when they get together in a group. It was actually very popular, a good laugh. Women loved it. Kids loved it. Obviously not the fellas so much. They came out of it rather badly.'

But women, too, were not slow in coming forward to let down the side. When the new series began filming, a real brawl erupted on set, between a mob of Glaswegian women and a gang of Essex girls. The fighting between them was real: they were pulling hair, spitting and yelling obscenities and eventually had to be pulled apart by the audience.

'I was terrified,' said a shocked Tarrant. 'It was mayhem. Two women started thumping each other and the rest just piled in. It was bizarre. I have never seen anything like it before, especially amongst women. Nothing like that has ever happened on the show before. They were hitting each other with stilettos. There was a lot of hair pulling and very unfeminine spitting. It was chaos. Jerry Springer might have big, burly security men, but we only had our weedy stage crew. I have no idea what sparked it. I was doing my bit in front of the camera when there was this shriek behind me. I turned around to see one woman clobbering another over the head with her stiletto. I don't know how they did it, but the crew finally managed to get them off stage and we stopped filming to let everybody calm down. Then we edited that bit out and just carried on.'

'Passions can get out of hand,' said a spokesman for the show with commendable understatement. They can indeed. But it was all grist to the mill and Tarrant wasn't worrying. For tomorrow belonged to him.

8

THE FULL CHRISSY

Tarrant was becoming used to unusual requests, but this one certainly made him sit up and take notice: would he accept £50,000 to take his kit off for *Cosmopolitan* magazine? No, he jolly well would not. Tarrant had enough common sense to realise that he risked overexposure as things were and to go for a full monty would just be that little step too far. Instead, he was concentrating on radio and television, with the emphasis on the former. He has often maintained that his true love is radio, rather than TV. 'People say, "I was fed up and you made me smile,"' he said. 'I find that far more satisfying and gratifying than doing a successful television show.'

And he continued to appeal to young and old. Indeed, he was keen to pull everyone in and, for his next stunt,

129

decamped to Cabot Square in London's Docklands for his early morning show. 'I can't wait to rope in a few bankers,' he said brightly. 'As usual, I'll try to cause a bit of chaos. With any luck the whole stock market should crash before lunchtime!' Now there's an example of separating the personal from the professional. Tarrant had and has significant stock market investments. The last thing he wanted was for the market to fall.

'I once got a six-figure tax bill and decided I didn't want to work so hard to earn so much money, only to give it all back again,' he explained. 'I started off looking into things like PEPs and bonds and that kind of stuff. Then I bought some shares – I bought shares at £1 in Capital Radio and sold them for £18. Then I started reading the *Financial Times* and it all went from there, really.'

Tarrant was pretty unwilling to give his hard-earned cash to anyone. He nearly got into serious trouble when he told a potential mugger, 'Go away please, or I'll slap you in the face.' Luckily for Chris, the youth did just that. 'I was cold and tired and told him I'd really rather be tucked up in bed,' Tarrant said afterwards. 'I said, "What's the point of me coming into work and handing my money over to a stranger?" It only dawned on me later it could have been nasty.'

In October 1997, even Tarrant's exuberance got the better of him. For his 51st birthday, Ingrid bought him a pair of bouncy boots: when trying them out, Chris crash-landed and broke his leg in two places. This was not good timing – there was yet another competition looming on the horizon as Zoe Ball was about to take over the breakfast show on Radio 1 (Evans had walked out in a huff). But there was no question at all of any long-term problem with the station: Tarrant proved his value to them beyond any shadow of a doubt.

In August that year Princess Diana was suddenly and tragically killed in a car crash: this had such a knock-on effect to just about every area of life that music stations actually suffered a fall in listeners as people tuned in to talk stations to hear the latest news. Capital was one of the many stations affected. But on top of that, at around this time, Tarrant had taken a five-week holiday. That also had an effect on the figures: the breakfast show lost 20 per cent of its listeners in the three-month period to September 1997. If Tarrant could have asked his audience to stage a graphic display of where Capital would be without him, he could not have done better himself.

That accident with the bouncing boots had an effect too – albeit a silly and rather trivial one. Chris had to cut back on his coffee consumption during the breakfast show because he couldn't go to the loo. 'With all the coffee he drinks, Chris usually goes to the toilet six times during the show,' confided an insider. 'Now he can't move so fast and has to do without his caffeine. It's driving him mad. We're taking bets on how long before he brings a potty in.'

Indeed, bodily functions were a far from taboo subject for Tarrant. He met one interviewer shortly after one morning show, who unwisely asked him if he'd managed to do all that was necessary after his three-hour stint. Tarrant took it in his stride. 'Have I had a crap?' he asked. 'No, I haven't had a crap. I had a poo-poo at ten past five this morning, thank you very much. And even if I hadn't – interesting fact this – pop records have got longer by approximately a minute a decade, which means there is plenty of time for a crap if I wanted one during the show. It's not the same thing at all if you work for Capital Gold. With your average 1.58 second Beatles track, there isn't time for a wee-wee, let alone a poo-poo. I used to have the office next door to Tony Blackburn and you'd see him rushing, hair flapping, to get back in time. It's why he always talks like "tha-aat". But with a George Michael anthem, I can have a shave, have a crap, make love to myself … Great questions of my life. Did I have a crap? What the fuck is it to do with you? I must remember to use that on the radio tomorrow.' It must be said – he had a point.

April Fool's Day was celebrated in a slightly less annoying way than the 1995 stunt: impressionist John Culshaw stood in for Tarrant for 90 minutes, while the real thing answered the phones. Quite a few of the listeners were fooled – but at least no one turned up for meetings they had already attended the week before.

An insight into Tarrant's working life came from his PA, Susan Willer, in 1997. Clearly something of a self-starter, it was actually she who persuaded him to take her on. 'I used to work at *TV-am* and loved it there but had to leave when it lost its franchise,' she recalled. 'The head of personnel there was a friend of mine so she let me know of a job going in Capital Radio's programming before it went up on the board. I went through the whole interview without knowing what the job was and it was only when I started that I realised it included looking after Chris Tarrant's mail. As I watched Chris walking around studying long lists, it soon occurred to me that he didn't have a PA. I persuaded him that there was so much I could do to free him up, from arranging his diary to selecting funny stories for the show. Capital were enthusiastic too, because now he could concentrate on being a TV and radio personality.

'I think what surprised me about him on our first meeting was how similar he was to the person on the radio. Some people have quite a different personality, but he was easy-going and friendly – almost paternal. In later years when I was going through a bad patch, he noticed and told me to take several weeks off to get things sorted out.

'He starts at 5am and I join him three hours later. From 8am until 10am I sit with him in the studio and while the records are spinning we work – it's the only time we have. The hours are perfect for me, which gives me some time with my little girl until she goes to bed, after which I have an hour for research. Chris always says thank you and, if I've worked particularly hard, he gives me a bottle of champagne.

'Compared with most of the presenters, Chris has a big team, including a producer, an engineer, a technical person

133

and me, but I do sometimes wish he was given a full-time researcher because I have to juggle this with the rest of my work. It is an intimate working environment. I've been here six years, but I am the newest member of the team. We all go on outings together and Chris takes us out for a treat twice a year. I'm friends with Chris outside of work too and often take my daughter to his house in Warwickshire for the weekend.' Clearly, Susan was someone who was very much in the 'with him' camp.

Chris, in turn, found life much more manageable with Susan on board. 'I had a huge volume of work and correspondence,' he said. 'When she was eventually assigned to work for me alone, I gave it all to her to attend to. This was when she became my PA within the company. That first week when I loaded her up with work she came back within a day and asked me if I had anything else to do. I found this was incredible and was convinced that she could not have done it properly. So I had to check it all and it was wonderfully correct.' And, of course, it left him even more time to pursue his other interests. Which he did.

He was still winning hands down over the competition. Chris Evans was doing the breakfast show on Virgin and Zoe Ball was *in situ* at Radio 1, but neither had anything like Chris's listening figures for the London area. Even the two of them combined couldn't knock him off his perch. In the first quarter of 1998, Tarrant attracted audiences of 2,035,000. Evans was getting 777,000 and Ball 529,000. And he was staying on his toes. Chris Evans brought the starting time of his radio show half an hour earlier to 6.30am: Tarrant countered by starting at 6am, which meant that he was broadcasting in the morning for an unprecedented four hours. He described the move forward just after the Evans announcement as a 'coincidence.' He was also enjoying every minute of it – and why not? He was winning.

'I like this competition thing,' he said gleefully. 'It keeps me sharp. There are 33 radio stations broadcasting in London, where once there were only five.' The comparisons with Evans, though, continued to irritate him. 'We're not at all alike,' he said. 'He's got ginger hair and glasses. I hate all this "Today's the big day" thing. How many more big days can me and Terry Wogan have? People think I'm holding Evans and Ball at bay but they're coming nowhere near me. Capital hasn't done a very good job of promoting us. They should hang our audience figures all over London.

'Evans's Virgin is number seven in London and frankly I'd find it depressing getting out of bed if my station was only number seven. Freud Communications has done a brilliant job in publicising Evans. Do I think he's good? I don't think anyone's as good as the hype.' Nor was he impressed by the zoo format. 'It sounds as if people are trying too hard to laugh at something that's not funny,' Tarrant continued. 'We introduced zoo very successfully in 1986. There is a danger if the chemistry isn't right. I quietly went back to doing my own thing.'

Nor was he particularly effusive about Zoe Ball, who he

claimed not to have heard of when she took over the Radio 1 breakfast slot. 'I think she's quite a talent, but I think she's in the wrong place,' drawled Tarrant. 'I think Radio 1 has seriously lost the plot. They are trying to be clever and arty. Because they're not interrupted by commercials, they could just do wall-to-wall hits in your ears like they used to. I choose the oldies that I play and that includes The Beatles and The Rolling Stones because they're part of the soundtrack of our lives. When I saw McCartney play live three years ago, the 18-year-olds in the audience knew the words of even the most obscure Beatles tracks.

'A lot of British bands, like Oasis, Pulp, Blur and the Lightening Seeds, are so derivative that I find it easy to enthuse about them. The 80s was a bit of a hard trawl with Kylie Minogue and Jason Donovan. But I think the music is incidental. When I hear a DJ say, "I'll let the music speak for itself," then I know they're really in trouble.'

The DJ's real rivals were, according to the man himself, Radio 4's *Today* programme and Radio 2's Terry Wogan, who were second and third in the London ratings respectively. 'Talk Radio and LBC haven't really taken off,' mused Tarrant. '*Today* is very good, but you get the City types switching to me after half an hour for light relief. In America, it's all big city radio. I did think about the Radio 1 breakfast show.

'I asked all my mates who worked there, Kenny Everett, David Jensen, Fluff Freeman, and they said I'd get a free hand for about a fortnight. Then one of the suits would say

that his wife had been driving through Ha[...]
didn't like what your man was saying.' And h[...]
adore the immediacy of radio. 'I can have an id[...]
at five to six and do it at five past and if it does[...]
can forget about it by ten past,' he said. 'If you have an id[...]
in television, you have to have four days of meetings and
analysis first.'

By now such an old pro, Tarrant could speak
knowledgeably about all aspects of broadcasting,
including advertising. It, too, had improved. 'Radio ads
are much better than they used to be,' said Tarrant. 'I
remember when I first started it was just hours of dry
speech, not even any jingles. It's important to have ads
that fit the style of the station.'

And he was popular with colleagues. 'He's held in high
esteem, a lot of success hangs on the breakfast show,' said
one. 'He's pretty well liked. It's recognised that he works
hard and he's not too proud to put a client's T-shirt on.'

In October 1998, Tarrant's personal life made a rather
unfortunate appearance in the press. He and Ingrid had been
having problems with Dexter, Ingrid's 17-year-old son from
her first marriage, and asked him to leave the house. The
story made national headlines because of the people
involved and because Dexter, who had gone to live with his
natural father, made a public attack on Chris. It was all the
more hurtful, because Tarrant had brought him up as his
own son.

'Dexter left school 15 months ago and we have worked

get him to look for a job,' said a weary
are sure many parents of teenagers will be
this problem. At the weekend, we insisted that,
was prepared to look for a job, he could no longer
the comfort of our roof over his head. It was entirely
his decision to go and live with his natural father. He is an
adult and must make his own way in the world. It's very sad
for any family when a teenage son chooses to leave home.
We have always treated Dexter as a member of our family of
six children and it's deeply hurtful for us that Dexter has
now chosen to use the high-profile Tarrant name in an
attempt to make money.'

Dexter was unrepentant. 'Chris had a real go at my dad
and I wasn't going to stand for it,' he said. 'We had a big
row about it and I basically said I was leaving. I went over
to my father's place and the next day I found they had got
all my stuff together, even my drum kit, and put it all in a
taxi and sent it over to my dad's house. From what I gather
my mum wasn't pleased but Chris didn't seem bothered I'd
gone. I've nowhere else to go so I'm staying here.'

As it happens, that was not really what happened.
Some years later, Ingrid told a rather different version of
the story. 'It wasn't Chris, it was me who booted him
out,' she said. 'Dexter was wasting his life. He needed
some tough love, so I packed his stuff in dustbin bags and
put them in a taxi to his dad's. All Chris did was support
me, saying, "Look, your mum's right. You can't expect to
have a roof over your head and everything provided for

you and you do nothing." He was right and Dexter understands that now. He's living with us again and playing drums in a band.'

It was an uncomfortable time for everyone and came at a turning point in Tarrant's life. For he had just been approached to front a new game show. The prize? It was to be one million smackeroos.

No one had ever done it before. Of course there had been game shows, some with very big cash prizes, but £1 million? It was quite a risk to take, not least because the only other show that had ever tried to offer something faintly comparable was *Raise The Roof* with Bob Holness. That programme had attempted to give away a £100,000 house every week, but didn't catch on and was axed after just one series.

The initial idea came from David Briggs, originally the flying eye reporter on Capital. And he had form: he became Tarrant's producer and came up with the competition *Double Or Quits* that was played on the breakfast show, and which was a poor man's version of *Millionaire*: the prize money started off at £1 and kept doubling. Briggs then teamed up with two friends who he'd met through Capital: Steve Knight and Mike Whitehill, who wrote advertising for Capital as well as comedy sketches for the likes of Jasper Carrott. It is that trio who get the royalties from the show.

'David, Mike and I first talked about a new game show four years ago,' said Steve in 1999. 'We had the idea of a quiz where you gamble and where the prize money doubles with each correct answer. We thought giving £1 million away was a magical figure. Our original title was *Cash Mountain*. We spent two years meeting now and again to talk about the format. We devised the three helplines, Ask The Audience, Phone A Friend and 50/50, to encourage people to gamble and not play safe, just sticking with the money they had won. But for 18 months we had meetings with various channels and no one was interested. We couldn't make a pilot because we'd have to give away prize money to get a real response from the contestants.'

But by this time they did have a programme maker. David Briggs approached Paul Smith, the founder and managing director of Celador Productions and Smith at once saw the potential of the show. 'This show was a passion of mine,' said Smith. 'When David Briggs first came to me, he didn't bring the format, he brought the mechanics, how the prize money would be created by using a premium phone line. He thought there would be questions and that the money would increase to a top prize – I think he even had £2 million and £5 million prizes, underwritten by insurance and with a newspaper partner to help us with publicity.' All of them began work on refining the format.

Once the format was designed to everyone's liking, Smith pitched the idea to ITV. On January 12 1996, he had a meeting with ITV Controller of Light Entertainment, Claudia Rosencrantz, at the ITV headquarters on Gray's Inn Road in London: she didn't like the name, *Cash Mountain*, but she did like everything else. 'The big twist was seeing the question before you make your mind up,' she said. 'It makes it seem easy. But it's not at all easy.'

However, it took some time before they could go ahead. Rosencrantz's then boss felt that, with *The Price Is Right* and *Family Fortunes* on board, they already had enough game shows and weren't looking for any more. 'That's why it took so long to come to air,' she said. 'I had to wait for a new director of programmes.'

That director came in the form of David Liddiment, who arrived in September 1997. Rosencrantz knew him from the days they had worked together at Granada in Manchester and was fairly sure he'd go for it. 'I told him about it immediately,' said Claudia. 'I knew him, I knew he would be willing to take a risk.'

The way she and Smith put the idea to him bordered on genius. Smith arrived with envelopes stashed with money – history does not record whether they were brown – and got Liddiment to play the game in real time, using Claudia as the phone a friend. It worked. Smith left the meeting without the money – which went to charity – but with a commission. Project *Millionaire* was ready to go.

You don't get a hit like *Millionaire* without some serious planning and that now swung in to action. For a start, the show set out to be 'classy, a game show for people who don't watch game shows'. So Smith brought in Pete Waterman, the man behind, amongst others, Kylie Minogue, to write the theme music, which the producers hoped would be a chart hit in itself. Andy Walmsley, the theatre and TV designer was brought in to fashion the set. Then Liddiment had another brilliant idea. 'David Liddiment had the brainwave of scheduling it on consecutive nights, which really helps to keep people tuning in,' said Steve Knight. Now all he had to do was to convince everyone else in the network. 'I knew it was a risk, but you try not to think about that,' Liddiment said.

Walmsley, meanwhile, set about constructing the set. When you tune in to a show like *Millionaire*, details like the set are taken for granted by the ordinary viewer, which is much as it should be because it looks, well, just right. In fact, an enormous amount of planning was involved, but Walmsley also had an enormous amount of scope. 'Most show budgets are declining at an alarming rate,' he said. '*Millionaire*'s was considerably larger. Therefore I could design something spectacular.'

He wasn't joking. The bowl shape of the set was based on the Riddler's lair in *Batman Forever*. 'Other details were borrowed from the courtroom scene in *Judge Dredd* and the incubation room in *Jurassic Park*,' said Walmsley. The initial budget for the set was £50,000, but the costs rose to £150,000, leading to the first series of the show making a loss on paper of £57,000.

There were an awful lot of complexities to sort out before the show went on air. For a start, the producers had to make sure they were operating completely within the gaming laws, where there is a thin line between a quiz show and a lottery. Phone lines had to be set up and a computer was built to generate the music. Questions and graphics had to be put in place. A presenter had to be found. This presented no problem at all.

Right from the start, Tarrant was the obvious choice. It was as if he'd spent the last 15 years on television earning this role, doing one dreadful show after another, until the time was finally right for him to have a massive hit. He had, as they say, paid his dues and, on top of that, he'd already worked with Smith on *Everybody's Equal*. And so in due course Tarrant signed on the dotted line for a £150,000 fee. The show was ready to roll.

Early reports, stemming from mid-1998, didn't really capture the excitement of what was to come. The press was told that contestants had to answer 15 questions correctly. 'There are no tricks or hidden obstacles,' said Chris. 'A person just needs skill, judgement and a steady nerve. And if they are struggling for a correct answer, I will even lend them a mobile phone so they can phone up friends and relatives to try and get the answer.' And that was the first ever hint of one of the three lifelines, Phone A Friend.

The first pilot was recorded on August 12, 1998, a month before the actual run was to start. It was a disaster. 'It looked like *Seaside Special* circa 1976,' said Smith. 'In spending so much time on the infrastructure, I'd taken my eye off the refinement of the TV structure. It's easy to forget it now, but I was ill with fear. The phone lines had opened and we were way below our projected revenue. At that point our predictions put us £400,000 in deficit. I had a meeting with the shareholders about three weeks before we aired. I told them this could either be our *Titanic* or our *Heaven's Gate.*'

Much to the discomfort of all concerned, Claudia Rosencrantz was there for the pilot. 'I know they wished I hadn't seen it,' she said. 'The basic grammar of the show worked. It still had 21 questions, starting at £1.' That £1 starter was clearly a mistake – Rosencrantz told them people would go off to make a cup of tea. 'Also,' she said, 'it didn't look right.' Smith got to his office the next day to find a letter from David Liddiment. 'I had a wonderful time last night,' it read. 'Somewhere in there you've got a great show. I'm sure you'll make it work.' Smith interpreted it thus: 'It's a complete mess. Get it sorted out or you'll never work again.'

And so, with less than a month to go before it aired, Paul Smith set out on a serious rethink. The mood had to become edgier, darker – after all, there was going to be an awful lot of money at stake. The set was toned down and stripped of some of its silver. The number of questions was brought down from 21 to 15. The music had to be changed.

That last decision was a serious risk. Pete Waterman is one of the most influential men in popular music and to replace him with a very, very different kind of composer required real courage. But something had to be done with the show – and fast. And so Smith engaged the services of Keith Strachan, with whom he'd worked on *Carrott's Commercial Breakdown.* Could he do anything? asked

Smith, having shown him the pilot. 'No,' said Strachan. 'But we can start again.'

And so Strachan and his son Michael set to work and composed something quite unlike the music of most game shows. It starts in C minor, rises by a semi tone for the next four questions and then two more progressions, each with its own tune, take it to a 'splendid tune in E for £1 million – a big bashing, Tchaikovsky ending, very camp', said Smith. 'Not that anyone will be listening at that point. They'll all be screaming their heads off.' It ended up as very unusual for the genre, with more than 100 pieces of music in all. The two men finished it in less than a week. 'The music was crucial,' said Smith. 'Take it out and you lose half the context.'

Having a now highly dramatic piece of music to work with, Smith next turned his attentions to the lighting. The lighting director was Brian Pearce, who had worked on the *Eurovision Song Contest* and the Barrymore shows. 'Be bolder,' was Smith's instruction. 'More attack. More bite. You have a completely open book. Tear up the conventions. I trust you. What do you need to make it more exciting?'

Pearce took him at his word. He decided to drastically lower the light levels, emphasising the overhead lamps that light the area where Tarrant and the contestant are sitting – what is known as 'giving it the *Mastermind*' in television jargon. The 220-strong audience was also carefully lit: light blue up to £1,000 and then progressively darker until, by the £1 million question, it was effectively black.

And to celebrate that £1 million win, if and when it ever came about, David Vialls, a visual effects designer, put together a package of fireworks, made up mainly of glitter cannons. Would anyone ever get that win? 'I think someone will do it,' said Tarrant after the first run. 'Some people are set on making TV history. They'll have watched a couple of series. They'll have strategies about how they'll use their lifelines. Someone will do it. And forget its effect on my career, it will be one of the best nights of my life. Bloody fantastic, it will be. The place will erupt. The roof will come off. It will be brilliant. We'll take a drink.'

Two days before the actual run, a second pilot was shot. Everyone was a bag of nerves – including the normally sanguine Tarrant. 'I've never seen so many nervous people,' he later recalled. 'Normally, I just swan into the studio. But that time, I took 15 minutes alone in my dressing room to get myself together. The expectation that someone would win £1 million on the first show was so great that this show could have been the biggest turkey of all time. It was a big gig for me – and for Liddiment. We were all as nervous as kittens.'

In the event, the second pilot was completely different from the first. Everything – the music, the lighting, the format – worked. Whittling the number of questions down to 15 made the contest much sharper and kicking off at a £100 win meant the audience was engaged from the start. Tarrant, needless to say, turned out to be the perfect presenter: he genuinely empathised with the contestants, put them at their ease in as much as anyone could be in that situation and, crucially, willed them to win. He also, however, proved adept at drawing out the tension.

It all ran to plan. The lucky winner walked away with £64,000 and left Smith in tears. It was going to be all right after all. One of the most successful game shows ever was about to go on air and, although no one realised quite how big it would become, everyone knew they had a hit. David Liddiment telephoned Paul Smith. 'This is the show we dreamed it would be,' he told him. 'It has delivered everything we dared hope it would.' *Who Wants To Be A Millionaire?* was on its way.

9

NOW EVERYONE'S A WINNER

The first run of the show was scheduled for September 4–13. It was to run every night for ten nights to create maximum impact and then, depending on the audience response, ITV would decide where next to take it. It was a gutsy decision on the part of David Liddiment, head of ITV. *Millionaire* would be up against both the *National Lottery* and *EastEnders*, each a formidable opponent on its own and together, a goliath. No matter. ITV was taking the risk. 'It's a brave move – it's never been done before,' said an ITV source.

'But people think the show could grip the nation. The whole concept of watching someone win or lose a million is massively exciting. Every night a clutch of ordinary people will be up there trying for the prize. Viewers will also be able to play at home, thanks to the multiple choice answer that will appear on the screen after each question. *EastEnders* is regularly in the top two of the TV chart. It would be tremendous if *Millionaire* made a dent in the ratings. People are likely to tape the soap and watch the quiz.'

And so, Tarrant settled into the usual publicity round, jovially defending his past programmes and talking happily about his career. 'Maybe these shows say something about the kind of guy I am,' he said cheerfully. 'My image is sort of "Jack the lad next door". Call it populist telly or something much worse, but it seems to get the ratings. I'm a pub sort of guy. My party piece is removing my pants before taking off my trousers. I used to think I was unique, then I saw Mr Bean do it.'

As the publicity machine swung into action, there was an air of increasing excitement. It began to sink in that on a game show, someone really could change their life. And, when the programme finally screened for the first time, the nation was transfixed. You'd have to have been on the planet Mars for the last five years not to know the format, but if that's the case, here goes: contestants have to answer 15 questions, each with four multiple choice answers, to win the prize.

Along the way they have three lifelines that they can use once each: Phone A Friend, Ask The Audience and 50:50, although more than one lifeline can be used per question. For the first, you can phone someone and have 30 seconds to read the question and possible answers and get a reply; for the second you ask the audience to choose an answer, they choose by remote control and you can see what percentage of the audience opted for which answer; and for the third, two incorrect answers are removed. Once you made it to winning £1,000 that sum would be guaranteed, as would £32,000. You could quit at any moment without giving an answer.

It immediately became apparent that this was gripping television. Viewers rang in in droves to take part in the next series – which was assured almost immediately – sparking the first of many rows that were to follow *Millionaire*, when it became apparent that the only people to have made a million were British Telecom. The firm earned at least that amount for the three million plus calls into the show, sparking 20 complaints to the telephone watchdog ICSTIS. But such rows were almost inevitable when you had a hit on your hands the size of *Millionaire*. And so at long last, nearly two decades after the end of *Tiswas*, Tarrant finally regained the television status that had once been his.

'We had no idea it would be so phenomenally successful, that it would strike such a chord with the nation,' said Steve Knight at the time. 'It's a show the whole family can watch – my three-year-old son Joseph loves it. Part of the success is also down to the contestants. They are randomly selected from the people who call in, so we get a genuine cross-section of society. That's a lesson to other game shows who audition their contestants to make sure they're bright, attractive and bubbly. We get some odd people on, but that's great! It means we get some people who don't win much, but I firmly believe someone will win £1 million. Everyone at the programme really wants to give away a million. I am sure that one day we will get the sort of person who does pub quizzes and knows everything and who is willing to gamble a lot of money.' They did get their millionaire, all right, but the first one was far from a person who does pub quizzes and was willing to gamble a lot of money ...

It didn't take long for another row to break out. This one centred on a decision to host a special edition of the show on Christmas Day 1998, which Christian charities objected to on the grounds it cheapened the spirit of Christmas. 'The Church doesn't want to be a wet blanket on this kind of thing,' said Steve Jenkins, a spokesman for the Church of England. 'But if people are encouraged to think they can solve their problems by appearing on a game show or winning the Lottery, then they almost certainly won't. Christmas is a time for families and thinking about life, God and truth. It is not about trying to win a million pounds on a tasteless TV show like this.'

The Christian Institute, which advises the government on social policy, was none too delighted either. 'Christmas is about being selfless and giving, like Jesus,' said deputy director Simon Calvert. 'It is not about winning lots of money. That sort of thing just shows that broadcasters are willing to contribute to the moral decline of the country. These Lottery-style giveaways undermine the work ethic and encourage people to believe in something for nothing.'

They were not alone in the criticism. The Catholic Church, Shelter and even the National Confederation of Parent Teacher Associations all joined in the condemnation but, of course, to no effect. ITV, delighted with the size of their success, had no intention of holding it over. '*Who Wants To Be A Millionaire?* has been a runaway success with 12 million viewers and we feel it will be a popular choice on Christmas Day,' said a spokeswoman. Tarrant himself agreed. 'I'm looking forward to it,' he said. 'It would be fantastic if someone won a million on Christmas Day.'

The New Year kicked off with yet more problems with the phone lines. This time round it emerged that callers who actually managed to get through and got four correct answers – potential contestants were quizzed just as the actual ones are – were then told they'd got it wrong even when they knew themselves to be correct. 'We have had a few problems with people who have a pulse rather than a touch phone,' said an embarrassed spokesman. 'Callers are given another number to ring if they have a pulse phone, but I think the problem is that they don't realise they've got one. Only a small number of people have experienced this.'

Certainly viewing figures were not affected. In early January 1999, *Millionaire* pulled in 17 million viewers, 62 per cent of the total audience. They were watching contestant Paul Beverley from Petersfield, Hampshire, go for the highest cash gamble to date: having won the £64,000 question, he gambled on £125,000 and lost, going home with only £32,000. Nonetheless, the programme makers were ecstatic. 'I am absolutely delighted with this figure,' said Tarrant,' *apropos* the ratings rather than Mr Beverley's win (or loss, whichever you prefer). 'The show has become a huge hit.'

You could say that again. The show was now making waves abroad, with one country after another expressing an interest in buying the format. This is where the serious money is made and, with at least 40 countries eager to sign up, the lucky original trio and programme makers Celador could scarcely believe their good fortune. 'The most effective option for the company has been to look at separate deals with different television firms in every continent,' said one ecstatic insider. 'It's a brilliant programme and there has been massive interest.'

And it was a show with a difference. 'The days of winning a car are long gone,' said David Liddiment. 'Big prizes are what the public wants.' It's what they were going to get too – but not yet. To date, the biggest prize had been £64,000, with a good deal of speculation within the industry that £1 million would never be paid out. As it happens – they were wrong.

It was not only Chrissy-wissy who was elated at the success of the show – it was just about everyone who was involved. ITV also had something to thank the Celador team for: due solely to *Millionaire*, it broke the BBC's stranglehold on weekend television ratings. For the first time in nearly two years, ITV came out on top, with *Who Wants To Be A Millionaire* beating every BBC prime-time programme on Saturday and Sunday nights.

ITV entirely failed to contain its glee: 'It is a tremendous success for us,' said an insider. 'We are cock-a-hoop to say the least. *Who Wants To Be A Millionaire* has been

NOW EVERYONE'S A WINNER

phenomenal – it keeps getting better and better. Our other programmes are building on that strength.' The BBC did what it often does when caught on the hop: it pointed its nose skyward and pretended not to care. 'We are not putting on a quiz show night after night,' said a spokesman sniffily. 'We strive to provide a diverse range of quality programmes.' It was just a shame the viewers didn't feel the same way ...

The success of the show was also attested to by the number of callers trying to get on. Over four million had phoned in by now, which meant that in January 1999, BT had made £1.7 million out of the calls and Celador had made £2 million. In fact, the only people who hadn't made a million out of it yet were the contestants, but that was to come in due course.

Millionaire fever was gripping the country. It wasn't just the desire to win a million that got people watching, it was witnessing the human drama taking place within the small screen. What would you do if you had got up to £125,000 and were not sure of the correct answer? Would you play safe or gamble to double your money, with the potential to lose half of it? Increasingly, it became apparent quite how clever those rules had been. And Tarrant himself was perfect as master of ceremonies: one moment teasing, the next drawing out the tension – he knew exactly how to extract every ounce of human emotion from that agonising multiple choice.

By February, the show had clearly become part of television history – and, remember, this was less than six months after the launch. Already features were appearing on past winners, who ranged, prize-wise, from £500 to £125,000. One of the men who won the highest prize to date was Martin Skillings. 'It changed my life, because I've paid my mortgage off and that's a biggie,' he said. There weren't that many television shows around responsible for changing people's lives and the wins didn't even have to be in six figures to do just that.

Lisa Hixson, a student, won £16,000 and that was quite enough for her. 'I owed about £6,000 in student loans – I'm appalling with money, which is how I got myself in such a mess,' she said. 'I burst into tears when I came off and I wasn't myself for two days. Just after the cheque cleared, I went to the cashpoint, and I was jumping up and down in the street when the balance came up. Then I put the card back in to see it all over again.'

The game fascinated everyone. Psychotherapist Arlene Gorodensky identified what she saw as the game's pull. '*Millionaire* is about winning money – the "It Could Be You" phenomenon,' she wrote. 'But this fortune winner has a deeper twist. Because it isn't just about answering questions, the psychological compulsion is not knowledge or luck: it is the issue of, to quote Chris Tarrant's catchphrase, "Are you sure?" It is the challenge of risking everything on self-belief. The quiz is set up to test contestants' inner certainty. The issue is their struggle to decide whether to trust themselves to get it right. And their trust is challenged throughout by Tarrant's questioning; by his querying eye; by the time lapse between question and acceptance; and by the audience's presence as a "supporter" whose alternate hope and fear turns the screw.'

Millionaire had become the most watched television show since Princess Anne's 1987 appearance on *Question Of Sport*. It was the 'quiz show for people who didn't watch quiz shows', it was the programme that had 'completely rewritten the rules of engagement for terrestrial television' – in short, it was a phenomena. No one involved had expected this to happen and no one involved seemed to be able to believe it. It had become that rarest of creatures, an STE, or Shared Television Event. So many people watched it that, come Monday morning, they were able to talk about it in the office and we hadn't seen the likes of that since the *Morecombe and Wise Christmas Special*, in the late 70s and early 80s. And that was when there were only three channels to choose from.

But still the pressure mounted for the show to produce that winner of a million pounds. There was even speculation that the programme might be dumbed down to get a winner, not least because the US networks, while clamouring for a slice of the action, also wanted a guaranteed jackpot. The makers refused to budge. 'I firmly believe the top prize will fall and Chris feels the same way,' said Adrian Woolfe, a spokesman for the show. 'We have no idea when it will happen, but one thing we are absolutely clear about is that there's no way we would make the questions easier just so we could get a millionaire.'

As public fascination with the programme grew, its

makers attempted to analyse what had made it such a success
– while appearing slightly dazed at their own good fortune.
'It's an awful expression, but it really is, "talk about" TV,'
said Mike Whitehill. 'The landlord of my local pub phoned
me at home when the first series was about three or four days
old and said, "I'd just like to say that everyone in the pub is
talking about it." For us, that was a dream come true.'

Another unusual aspect of the programme was that, once
the contestant had been picked, the game started almost
immediately, with little banter between contestant and host.
It worked well, although there had been concerns about it.
'When we were discussing the programme, we were worried
about wanting to get on with the game, since the audience at
home wouldn't really care about the contestants because they
didn't know enough about them or their family background,'
said Whitehill.

'But that wasn't, as it happened, the case, because people
made snap judgements, such as, "I really want him to win,"
or "He's a bit big for his boots." In the same vein, the
amounts of prize money were less important than we
thought. Of course, £125,000 winners make headlines. But
people's aspirations to wealth are very different. For one
person, £1,000 might be a lot of money and they'd be happy
to take that.'

As for the questions themselves, they were stored in a huge
computer away from the studio, and fed into the studio
during the show. And, in those early days, problems
sometimes arose there too. Celador was hugely embarrassed

when, in March 1999, contestant Tony Kennedy gave a wrong answer – and won. He had got to £64,000 when the following question came up: 'Theoretically, what is the minimum number of strokes with which a tennis player can win a set?'

Kennedy answered 24 and was judged a winner: only afterwards did everyone realise that the right answer was 12 and so his winnings should be only £32,000. 'Having reviewed tonight's question regarding the minimum number of strokes with which a tennis player can win a set, we recognise that within a particular situation this can be achieved with 12,' said a spokesman for the company. 'We operate a rigorous procedure involving three points of reference for verifying each question. We are investigating how this procedure has failed to ensure that a similar mishap does not occur again.'

Barely had the show recovered from that when something happened that was almost worse. Another contestant, Sheridan Booth, who won £500, turned out to have been in prison, which contravened the rules of the show. His offence was for theft – and worse still, it emerged that he'd kicked a puppy to death. The show promptly froze his winnings, but the point was made that such was the interest in *Millionaire* that nothing like this could be allowed to happen again. The programme makers began to hold emergency councils about what to do.

Given the intensity of his schedule, it was hardly surprising that Tarrant had a bed installed in his sitting room to take the odd catnap during the day. 'I'm living on four hours sleep plus a bit in the daytime,' he said cheerily. And, perhaps unsurprisingly, the show began to win the first of many awards: the Royal Television Society's prestigious Entertainment Programme of the Year award.

Now optioned in 31 countries, the show was sweeping the board as far as international awards were concerned, let alone the domestic variety. *Millionaire* won six major awards at the Montreux International Television Festival, an unprecedented triumph, including Best Game Show award for Tarrant himself.

And at last an American deal was on the cards. Avesco Communications was known to be in talks with the US channel ABC about a potential buy-up of the format, a deal that could be worth millions to all concerned. Avesco owned the rights to the show through its associated company Complete Communications, which in turn owned Celador. 'If this attracts the interest in America that it has done in the UK, then it could be worth millions,' said one Avesco insider, scarcely able to conceal his excitement.

Meanwhile, Tarrant himself was reaping the rewards of the show's success. Quite apart from the money he made presenting the programme – by this time he had negotiated a £2.5 million deal to continue hosting the show into the new millennium, with a rollover contract for 27 shows in 1999 and 44 the following year – his profile was higher than ever and yet more promotional activity was flooding in. By this time estimated to be earning about £4 million a year, latest

NOW EVERYONE'S A WINNER

up was a deal with Jacob's, the Cream Cracker people, which featured both Tarrant personally and *Millionaire*.

The ubiquitous Cream Crackers, Twiglets and Club biscuits would all feature both as sponsors of the show and bearing Tarrant's cheery mug on their packaging. 'There will be mentions of Jacob's products in much the same way that Cadbury flashes up at the beginning, middle and end of *Coronation Street*,' said an ITV source. 'And Chris will appear on packets of Cream Crackers and other Jacob's biscuits, cross promoting the programme. Negotiations have been tough, but they have been concluded successfully.'

Sheridan Booth, the convicted criminal who had won £500 and then turned out to have kicked a Labrador to death was not the only problematic contestant on the show: two more, Neil Muir and Andrew Lavelle, also had criminal records and like Booth had signed forms stating exactly the opposite.

Muir, a builder from Wallasey, Merseyside, had won £64,000 the previous January, and then turned out to have convictions for theft, deception and forgery. Lavelle, meanwhile, from Wrexham, who won £16,000 in March, actually appeared on the show while he had a warrant out for his arrest in connection with hundreds of pounds of unpaid fines including driving while disqualified, obstructing the police and breaching a community service order. In all three cases, viewers rang into the show to complain about the winnings. The programme makers' decision was really their only option. 'We welcome everyone to the show, but anyone with a criminal record will simply not get away with it,' said a clearly relieved Paul Smith.

And so, at long last, *Millionaire* debuted in the United States. Just as it had been in Britain – and it used exactly the same format, right down to the music – it was an instant runaway success. The host in this case was one Regis Philbin, who the *New York Times* lost no time in comparing unfavourably to the English version. 'He is following Mr Tarrant's lead ... pawing the women just as the British host does,' it wrote. Tarrant's people were sniffy. 'It's a completely ridiculous statement,' said one. 'Unfortunately you can't sue everyone who slags you off.'

As the search for that elusive *Millionaire* winner continued – and there were an awful lot of complaints from jealous rivals that the top prize would never be paid out – Celador pointed out that in actual fact the show was nearing the £1 million mark in terms of prizes won: £840,000 by the end of its first full year. On top of that, a total of ten million would-be punters had called in trying to get on the show – and at an average spend of 77p per call, BT and Celador were doing very nicely.

And the winners themselves – or at least those without a criminal record – continued to enchant. Jonathan Green, a fireman who won £250,000, could not have been better PR for the programme. Married to Nicky, with five sons, the 50-year-old, who lived in Doddinghurst, Essex, was adamant that he would not be giving up the day job. 'I know it sounds terrible, but it's not that much,' he admitted. 'I haven't really thought about all the ways it will affect our life yet. It's still sinking in and I'm keeping all my options open. I will leave the money in the bank until I calm down.'

He followed that up by revealing that some of his winnings would be going to his two eldest children from his first marriage, his parents and Noel Diancono, his dial-a-friend, who helped him with the question: 'What lives in a formicary?' The answer was ants. 'The one person I knew I needed on my side was Noel, because of his good grasp of general knowledge,' said Jonathan, as the two were pictured sipping champagne with Tarrant. Noel himself, an out-of-work actor who had been the chauffeur at Jonathan's wedding, was equally appealing. Admitting to being in a state of 'structured panic' when the call came through, he said the money provided just the boost he needed. 'I have been given all I hoped for and a little more,' he said. 'But I must say it was scary when he called me. There was so much riding on it and I didn't want to drop a friend in it.' In the event, it worked out well for everyone – not least Celador, who were now making the questions that little bit more difficult as callers continued to wise up.

One person who was watching the proceedings with a fairly jaundiced eye was one Chris Evans. Evans, the young pretender, had still not managed to unseat Tarrant from his throne, and he was clearly determined to try to steal some of his rival's glory. And so, unusually for him at the time, he started a stunt that never really took off – perhaps because he was using someone else's idea rather than his own. He announced that he would give £1 million to a viewer of his (then) hugely popular programme *TFI Friday*, following that up for good measure by giving away a further £1 million on his Virgin morning radio show. The prizes would be guaranteed.

The idea was this. So far, despite the hype, no one had actually won £1 million on Tarrant's show. Evans, therefore, would come up with the real thing and really give a huge sum of money away. 'Someone is going to be a millionaire – a Millennium millionaire,' he said. The slot would run between September and Christmas Eve, when Evans would call a Virgin listener. 'If we call your number and you answer in fewer than five rings, "Morning, Christoph, I am so excited I have to go to the toilet," I will ask you three questions,' Evans announced.

'Get two out of the three right and you will win £1,000, which you can keep or which you can exchange for a ticket to win a million. Then on Christmas Eve, all the names of the people with tickets to win a million will be fed into a computer that morning on the breakfast show. One of those names will be chosen at random and called. If that person once again answers two questions out of three correctly they will win £1 million tax free. If they don't we'll be calling somebody else, and somebody else and somebody else until someone becomes a millionaire.'

In the event that is exactly what happened, but it caused none of the sensation Evans obviously wanted to provoke. What he hadn't taken into account was that the tension had been building on *Millionaire* in two ways – both within every show for each contestant and overall as the search for that overall winner continued. Evans was really running little more than a lottery, which was a pale imitation of something that was becoming a national obsession. The result was something of a damp squib.

But it was certainly the case that the lack of a millionaire winner was giving rise to accusations that the show was carefully designed never to produce a winner. Even the show's bosses themselves were becoming concerned. 'Four series in a row without a millionaire certainly isn't what we envisaged,' said one source. 'We'll be looking closely at the format, although we are reluctant to make the questions easier.'

Even the controller of BBC1 had something to say. Peter Salmon watched his own station's ratings plummet to just 1.9 million viewers during one showing of *Millionaire*, just nine per cent of the audience and the station's worst night since 1946, prompting him to launch an astonishing attack on the show. 'It is an out and out commercial proposition,' he snapped. 'It starts with sponsorship, then you have got to pay to use those phone lines. If you are not careful, it can replace all those things we cherish and want to keep alive as well.' Unsurprisingly, ITV dismissed the comment as a 'case of sour grapes'.

By the end of 1999, just 12 months after the show began, it was ready to start on its fifth series. Most of the nation now seemed to be talking about it – and yet still no millionaire had been made. No matter – it still made gripping viewing, and the longer it went on, the greater the chances of that win finally happening. 'We want the million to be won and the odds seem to indicate that it's likely to be won,' said Paul Smith. 'In series one the highest prize was £64,000. In series two we broke the £125,000 barrier and in series four we broke the £250,000 barrier.'

Of course, as the show went on and viewers became accustomed to the format, many were beginning to devise a strategy to go about winning. Increasingly it was clear that, even if you didn't actually win £1 million, £250,000 was not a bad compensation prize – on top of which, as each series produced a still bigger winner, the kudos of becoming the first person to win £1 million grew ever greater. Smith was delighted that the highest prize in each series was getting bigger. 'I think there's a variety of reasons,' he said. 'In the last series we saw contestants who were very serious about where they were going. They were there to win as much money as possible. They had worked out their tactics in advance, as far as they were able, given the uncertainty of the questions.'

Ironically, this in itself could cause problems. A gambler who threw it all away made for better television than a cautious scholar who preserved a decent five-figure prize. 'They were quite determined to go for their goal and forget the unwritten contract they have with us, which is to be a bit entertaining when they're getting there, please,' said a good-humoured Smith. 'Some of them were just so focused they were monosyllabic. I'm not complaining, if that's the way they want to play then it's their business, but I think it's evident that the contestants are learning to play better. I don't know quite what has made it [*Millionaire*] touch the nation as much as it has. I can only say it's serendipity – it just happened to be in the right place at the right time. When *Millionaire* was getting 68 per cent [of the viewing figures] and audiences of 19 million, it was far beyond anything we could ever have imagined.'

And for Tarrant, it was a welcome distraction from another part of his life. Many years earlier he had worked with Sophie Rhys-Jones, now Prince Edward's fiancée. In the spring of 1999, it was a relationship that made headlines all over the world.

10

A RIGHT ROYAL STITCH-UP

From her very first days as Prince Edward's girlfriend, Sophie Rhys-Jones attracted comment because of her working relationship with Chris Tarrant. The Prince and the PR girl was already an unusual coupling but, given the fact that the PR girl's clients included not only Chris Tarrant but Noel Edmonds's creation Mr Blobby, interest in Sophie's past was always present. And right from the start there were rumours, always fiercely denied, that she and Tarrant had had a brief relationship. Tarrant had, in fact, already met Ingrid when he and Sophie worked together, but it was an entertaining notion, just the same.

Nor was Sophie a typical Royal girlfriend. She came from stolid middle-class stock: born in Oxford and brought up in Kent in a farmhouse in Brenchley, near Tunbridge Wells, where she lived with her parents Christopher and Mary and her brother David. Christopher worked in the automotive business, later becoming a commodities broker, while her mother earned extra money through typing. The family was comfortable but not rich: Sophie needed to work in her early days to support herself. Not for her a trust fund or rich daddy; rather, she'd been a working girl, plain and simple, and back in 1994, when she and Edward first became an item, she had to continue to work.

Spotted at the charity Baby Lifeline early on in the relationship, Royal watchers happily speculated that, as a Royal-to-be, she was already involving herself in charitable work. This was not the case. 'I am not the president or patron of the charity,' said Sophie to one reporter. 'I actually do real work. It is not just waving to photographers.' Her colleagues and friends nodded vigorously in agreement – amongst them one Chris Tarrant, who engulfed Sophie in a hug. 'I always like to help Sophie,' he beamed.

And so Sophie and Chris got on with their lives: Sophie building up her own PR firm and Tarrant becoming one of the most successful broadcasters in Britain until finally, after many years of speculation as to whether they would even actually get married, Sophie became engaged to Prince Edward in 1999. Everyone was delighted and there was immediate conjecture as to whether Tarrant would be invited to the wedding. There also surfaced, not for the first time, a rumour about a photograph of the two of them together. One newspaper wrote, 'Former colleagues are said to possess an amusing photograph of her sitting on his knee.' But no matter. It was all a long time ago – eight years, to be precise – and no one seemed to be that interested in something so innocuous.

Except that it soon turned out that the photos were not that innocuous after all. In fact, they weren't innocuous at all. Sophie was actually topless in the pictures, giving rise yet again to speculation about the real nature of her relationship with Tarrant, to say nothing of severely embarrassing both her and the Royal Family. For years Sophie had been cultivating a demure image, in marked contrast to those of the late Princess Diana and the Duchess of York, but there was nothing very demure about hopping around with your top off with a middle-aged, married DJ. Sophie spoke about her 'remorse' over the pictures. Everyone involved pretty much hoped the issue would go away.

Perhaps they were naïve – or perhaps they really did believe that no one would be unkind enough to publish. Of course, both Tarrant and Sophie had known about the picture for years, but Tarrant had given his assurance to Sophie that she wouldn't have to worry about it because he clearly believed that to be the case. Kara Noble had done the same. But, of course, there is an enormous market for anything involving the Royal Family behaving in a less than decorous fashion and so it was really only a matter of time before the picture appeared. And it did.

It was the *Sun* who bought the offending picture from its owner, none other than Kara Noble. Less than a month before the wedding was due to take place, the *Sun* published the snap: taken after a Capital Radio broadcast from Spain in 1988, it showed an embarrassed Sophie turning away from the camera as Tarrant lifted up her bikini top. Alongside, under the heading 'He Was Under Sophie's Spell', it ran lurid claims about the true nature of her relationship with Tarrant.

Kara Noble talked about the 'strong chemistry' between the two of them. In the five pages of what the *Sun* termed 'star Tarrant's sexy fun with Edward's bride', Noble continued, 'It was clear that Chris was attracted to her. He gave her more of his time. I felt an unmistakably intense flirtation between them.'

There was an awful lot more where that came from. After revealing that Sophie first met Chris when she was just 21 in 1986, she continued, 'There were some people who believed that the flirtation had moved on to a deeper level and they would ask me about it. But I adored Chris and liked Sophie and would never be drawn into the gossip. It was taken for granted, though, that Sophie and Chris shared a special closeness – it was just accepted as being the way it was. It wasn't considered a big deal – they were two popular people who we all liked and it was just nice that they shared something special. But their flirtation did raise eyebrows at times, mine included.

'There was no doubt that Chris was under Sophie's spell and she made no secret of the fact that she thought he was the bee's knees. There was a feeling of infatuation about the way they behaved with each other, a friction of unmistakable attraction and a remarkable undercurrent of intimacy. There was an unspoken agreement among the staff that Chris and Sophie shared something special – they were almost reverential about it. Chris was putty in her hands and she was always starry-eyed around him. They got on tremendously well together.' And, just in case anyone had missed the point, Noble then talked about an occasion when Sophie sat on his knee, with the two of them cuddling. And so it went on. And on. And on.

Poor Sophie was absolutely devastated. She spoke of her 'deep, deep hurt' and added, 'This has ruined my engagement. This was supposed to have been the happiest time of my life.' Prince Edward, meanwhile, called it a 'disgusting act'. Everyone around her was quick to agree. She had been only 23 when the picture was taken, it was years before she had even met Prince Edward and it was even clear from the snap that she had not been altogether happy about the pose.

Meanwhile, there was an immediate show of public support for Sophie, while at the same time Kara Noble and the *Sun* were widely condemned. Indeed, there was real anger in some quarters. 'This was an act of boisterous tomfoolery by Chris that went too far,' said a friend of Sophie's, speaking with her consent. 'Sophie was not compliant, but here she was, a young woman of 23 working for a famous – and famously high-spirited – disc jockey. It is monstrous that it should come back and haunt her, virtually on the eve of what should be the most satisfying time of her life. Sophie is very, very upset by what has happened. She never believed in her wildest dreams that this picture would ever be shown in public.'

It turned out that the picture had actually been taken by Kara Noble, as the three were driving back to their hotel in Spain. It also emerged that Kara had told Sophie she had nothing to worry about and that the picture would remain private. 'Sophie was assured this was the case,' the friend continued. 'She was given a commitment that it would never see the light of day. She told me she feels utterly betrayed, she is distraught about it, desperately so. She told me, "Kara assured me she would never sell it. How could she cash in?"'

Sophie actually found out what was about to happen one evening when she was dining out with friends. She immediately returned to Buckingham Palace to ask for help – and got it. Prince Edward was said to be 'livid'. Tarrant himself was embarrassed and upset – not least because the picture didn't show him in quite the best light. However, he dismissed it as 'high jinks' and nothing more. 'Chris is a great one for cuddling everyone in the studio,' said a friend. 'It's all part of his style and is always totally innocent.'

Tarrant himself felt so angry that he read out a public statement on his Capital breakfast show. It read as follows:

As a journalist myself, I am so sad this morning. I am so horrified that this sort of garbage, this sort of vindictive, dreamed up nonsense, is still being bought and allowed to be printed in our newspapers in this country. OK, there is a picture of Sophie Rhys-Jones taken with me – I think it was actually at least nine years ago, it might have been ten – topless, when we were all mucking about as loads of young guys do, loads of young girls do, in the Spanish sunshine on a Capital outside broadcast. So what? So what? Is this a moralistic judgement? This is from the paper that first introduced the topless model to all our newsstands every morning. These are the people who invented Page 3.

Sophie is, and was, a great laugh. Really good fun. A great extrovert. Full stop! She was always a totally moral, really decent girl. Nothing immoral happened between us, before or after this picture. This picture has been hawked around Fleet Street to the highest bidder for months. The picture is just a bit of a giggle. There must be thousands of young girls in this country – genuinely just young British girls away on holiday – who have got pictures like this in their private collection. And that's all it was. It was in somebody's private collection, who suddenly decided to sell it for the maximum amount of money they could get. No matter who they hurt, that's what they decided to do to sop up their bank account. There was no doubt whatsoever who that last was aimed at – Kara had reportedly got £100,000 for the picture – and Tarrant had more to say on the subject. 'For the person who sold this picture and made up – and you know you did make up – this totally fabricated story, that you sold for as much money as you could possibly get from a tabloid newspaper, I don't even feel anger,' he went on. 'I don't feel disgust. I just feel hugely betrayed at first, and I'm sure Sophie does. But above all I just feel a deep sadness. Kara, how far down have you gone? How will you live with yourself? How will you ever, ever face any of us at Capital? And how will you ever face Sophie again?'

It was strong stuff and others were quick to agree. The Queen herself, no less, called the publication of the picture 'premeditated cruelty' and totally condemned the lurid account of Sophie and Tarrant's relationship. 'This morning's story in the *Sun* is a gross invasion of privacy and cannot be regarded as in the public interest,' said a Palace statement. 'It has caused considerable distress. Prince Edward and Miss Rhys-Jones are very grateful to those members of the public who have telephoned offering support, which naturally is also our immediate concern. We shall, of course, be considering further action and no options have been ruled out.'

She was backed by Tony Blair. In what must pretty much have been a first, the monarch and her Prime Minister both rose to the support of a PR girl. 'The Palace have said what they have said and, yes, we agree with that,' said a Number 10 spokesman. 'Freedom of the press is very important but with that freedom comes responsibility and it's important that, when the media exercise that freedom, you show judgement.

It was rapidly becoming clear to everyone that the publication of that photograph had been a massive mistake. After some urgent consultations within News International, *Sun* editor David Yelland issued an apology. 'We clearly upset

Miss Rhys-Jones,' he said. 'It's clear to me that we have caused her great distress. I have therefore decided to apologise to her and to the Palace. I believe this is the right thing to do. No more topless pictures of Miss Rhys-Jones will appear in the *Sun*. I wish her and Prince Edward the very best, although I don't expect to be invited to the wedding.'

It was too little too late and the flippancy of the end of that comment left quite a few people with the impression that he might have been sorry, but he wasn't *that* sorry. Nor did it help when it emerged that he'd sent his staff an e-mail, denying that he would be sacked over the fiasco, saying, 'They can't get rid of me that easily.' Kara Noble was not so lucky. As the Palace lodged a complaint with the Press Complaints Commission, she paid the greatest price of all: she was sacked from her job at Heart FM.

Richard Huntingford, director of Chrysalis, which owns Heart FM, was livid. 'We are shocked and disappointed that Kara Noble has betrayed the trust of Sophie Rhys-Jones and everyone here at Heart,' he said. 'Her actions are completely at odds with everything that Heart stands for.' Kara's fellow presenter Jonathan Coleman was none too impressed, either. 'I would find it hard to look Kara in the eye,' he said.

Support for Sophie was widespread. Her business partner, Murray Harkin, revealed that she had taken the day off work because she was so upset and had been receiving huge numbers of messages from the public. 'She has been inundated by calls via Buckingham Palace from members of the public and they have been very supportive,' he said. 'It's such a distressing thing to happen so near to the wedding. It should be the happiest time of their lives for her and for Prince Edward. I think Edward has been deeply supportive.'

And as the events surrounding the publication of the picture emerged, Kara was shown in an increasingly bad light. A plan to buy the picture to save Sophie's blushes had been mooted a few months earlier: Richard Huntingford had apparently offered to buy the picture from Kara Noble, paying the money to a charity of her choice. But it was Sophie herself who turned the plan down. 'If I can't trust Kara, who can I trust?' she said. 'If we try to buy the photograph, it looks like a cover-up and I have nothing to hide. I do not want people paying for these photos on my behalf – it will look like hush money.'

Ingrid Tarrant stepped into the furore. 'There was never a relationship between Sophie and Chris – despite the heavy hints in the *Sun*,' she said. 'We knew this photograph was floating around and Chris swore to me, on his son's life, that there never had been anything between them. That's not something you do lightly. It would be tempting providence. Anyway, I never suspected there was a relationship. I knew Sophie as well and I would have known if anything was amiss.'

She didn't stop there. The full extent of the Tarrants' disgust at Kara's actions became clear as she continued, 'Chris feels let down and betrayed by a former colleague. She's obviously a very bitter woman. She's unloved, unwanted, unmarried and uncaring. Chris and I are terribly saddened by the whole thing. The photo itself was just silly, fun behaviour. We have all done it and had it done to us. Why not? It's good to have fun. I will be contacting Sophie to offer her my support and tell her we are totally cool about the whole thing. But it was an awful thing to print the photo so close to her wedding. It's spoiled her engagement. It would spoil anyone's. This incident happened during an outside broadcast in Spain. There were a lot of other people there too. But I guarantee no one except this woman Kara will be coming out with any nonsense about Chris and Sophie. They don't deserve this. They are both decent people.'

In fact, Tarrant was so furious that the row even spilled over into *Millionaire*. There were rumours that he might stand down as presenter of the show – because it was sponsored by the *Sun*. 'Chris is very, very angry,' said a friend. 'He's made it clear that he'd find it hard to have his name closely linked with the paper that caused so much hurt and damage.' Celador was worried, but there was nothing it could do. 'It is not down to us – this sponsorship arrangement is made between ITV and the paper,' said spokesman Adrian Woolfe. 'We have absolutely no comment on any aspect of this matter.'

Tarrant was also scathing about the *Sun*'s apology. 'I take no pleasure from the apology,' he said. 'It is the fastest, most humiliating back pedal by any national newspaper I have ever seen. These photographs, this story, should never have been up for sale in the first place. It's a very sad business. It's very rough on me and my kids. The bottom line for the two people who love each other, who are getting married in two weeks' time, is for God's sake leave them alone. They have done nothing, they're harmless, they are nice people. There are no skeletons in their cupboard so leave them alone. Give them a break. What happened to the new code of morality we were supposed to see after Diana died? I see no sign of that. It was a dreadful story. The timing was appalling. The *Sun* completely misread the situation. Leave Sophie alone.'

All of which left the obvious question: why on earth did Kara Noble do it? Money might have been one incentive, but £100,000 doesn't really compensate for losing your job, your lifestyle, your reputation and your future. Indeed, as the first flashes of anger began to die down, everyone began paying rather more attention not to the woman who was actually in the pictures, but to the woman who took them.

Kara was labelled a Judas, a good-time girl, a woman who habitually lied about her age and had a string of toy boys. She herself had gone abroad to escape the fuss, but she was going to have to come back one day and, the way it was looking, she was going to have a very hard time. But initially, it seemed, it really was the money.

It was not actually the main participants who began delving into her past. Throughout the uproar Sophie had been advised by her old boss Brian MacLaurin, who publicly announced that the Prince and his bride-to-be had forgiven Kara. 'Sophie has seen the level of public opinion directed against Kara with headlines like "slapper", "Judas" and "traitor", and she wants it to stop,' he said. 'Sophie has spoken to Chris and they are all aware that Kara is being followed by the media. While Sophie and Edward remain very upset about what happened, they think it is time to move on. They think she has suffered enough and she should not be hassled. Sophie is well aware of what it is like. Kara was stupid and silly and misguided, but she is not a traitor.'

But the media had scented blood and it wasn't Sophie's. When anyone is unlucky enough to have the press in full pursuit, it is not easy to calm them down, as Kara was beginning to find out. A picture of her in a basque, stockings and high heels was published everywhere. Her finances were raked over with a toothcomb: she was said to be in money troubles, with a tax demand of £11,000 on its way and an overdraft of £3,000. Dark hints were raised that in the past she'd had trouble paying her mortgage, as well as another £27,000 tax demand. It was even hinted that in reality her salary was much less than the widely reported £100,000.

'Getting her own show inflated her ego and her spending patterns,' said one colleague. 'She felt she had to live up to the image. She bought an expensive house in a fashionable area of west London. I'm sure that put extra financial pressure on her. Also, at Capital she earned a lot of money doing voice-overs and adverts. At Heart, her profile dropped and she was not getting as much work.'

Another colleague said much the same. 'She didn't have anything like as many listeners as she did at Capital,' he said. 'After a while, she was struggling to get bookings for celebrity appearances that pay very well. Promoters and public-relations people were thinking, Kara who? Ironically, everyone knows who she is now, but no one will touch her with a bargepole. She had put together a glossy brochure of her company KN Productions and was pitching for a TV show on Channel 4 comparing US DJs and UK DJs. She will hear in a week if that is successful but, if I was Kara, I wouldn't hold my breath.'

There was a good deal more of this before her private life came under scrutiny. That was even worse. More pictures of her emerged flashing her stockings and sitting on Peter Stringfellow's knee. Colleagues recalled that she quite frequently flashed her breasts and even performed a lap dance. Perhaps worst of all, though, was an account of her actions given by Andrew Nunn, a chef with whom she'd had a brief fling a couple of weeks before the publication of the photos, which made the whole escapade appear utterly callous and premeditated.

Stating that Kara had a 'huge ego', Andrew began, 'It was obvious she's jealous that Chris Tarrant preferred Sophie to her. She thinks Sophie's a dull, plain girl and I don't think she could understand why Chris liked Sophie more than her. There was obviously no love between her and Sophie. She didn't even seem to regard her as a friend. Kara couldn't believe Chris fancied Sophie and not her because she was in great shape and she used to be his radio co-presenter. She obviously has feelings for Chris and was jealous of Sophie.'

A very vivid picture of a woman scorned was beginning to

emerge – which also explained her venom at the expense of Chris after leaving Capital. That, in fact, was a much more plausible explanation for her actions than merely needing the money, especially after it emerged that she was furious not to have been invited to the wedding.

She said she planned to 'throw a spanner in the works', said Andrew, recalling a walk the two of them took in the country. 'Kara was furious she hadn't been invited. She had been snubbed and she wanted to get back at Sophie. She kept taking calls on her mobile as we talked. She told me it was her lawyer and she was negotiating to sell the topless pictures of Sophie for £100,000. She said the picture would be published a week or two before the wedding. The timing seemed to be calculated to cause maximum chaos. I didn't really take her seriously. I thought she was just making up a story to impress me.'

But, as the two spent more time together, it became apparent that she was quite serious, asking Andrew to keep quiet about the picture, and telling him that she had needed someone to confide in. 'Kara had it all worked out in detail,' Andrew continued. 'She was very het up and nervous the whole time. She told me she was going to quit the radio station and use the money to set herself up with her own show, possibly in Los Angeles. She said she was sick of being a sidekick. Jono seemed really nice but Kara said he was a motor mouth who hardly let her get a word in. She said she wanted her own show. She wanted relatives of dead people to call in and request the dead person's favourite song. It all seemed nutty to me. She didn't seem at all bothered that she would be ruining Sophie's wedding. Kara said the wedding was a farce. She was convinced that the marriage is just good public relations for the Royals after the death of Diana.'

Of course, Tarrant himself didn't emerge particularly well out of this. It might have been a bit of larking about that got out of hand, but exposing a young woman's breasts is not really all that funny, even if she did manage to take it in good heart. It gave credence to all those complaints that Tarrant could be a bit of a boor where women were concerned and could not always be relied upon not to overstep the mark. It was an unfortunate time for all concerned.

Nor did it blow over quickly. The row had been so heated and so intense that it was to simmer on for weeks, bringing even the very nature of the freedom of the press into the debate. The villains of the piece were clearly David Yelland, the *Sun* and, of course, Kara Noble, and the rest of the country lost no time in telling them so. In early June, the Press Complaints Commission issued a serious rebuke to the *Sun* – so much so, in fact, that Buckingham Palace felt justice had been done and said it would not be pursuing its own complaint.

Certainly, the Commission felt the matter had been extremely serious, not least because the paper had broken the industry's code of practice. This really was a concern, especially as the newspaper industry has always argued that self-regulation is preferable to government legislation when it comes to what papers can and cannot print, and actions like the *Sun*'s ended up threatening the freedom of every newspaper.

'It cannot be acceptable simply to break the code one day and apologise the next,' said Lord Wakeham, chairman of the PCC. 'The newspaper's apology in no way excuses the grave error which was made, nor lessens the distress which it caused Miss Rhys-Jones. The decision to publish these pictures was reprehensible and such a mistake must not happen again.' David Yelland, who by now must have been wishing he'd never heard the name Sophie Rhys-Jones, was forced to apologise yet again.

Never one to miss an opportunity to aim a kick in the direction of Tarrant, Chris Evans chose this moment to step into the fun. There had been rumours that Ingrid Tarrant had been offered Kara's job on Heart FM and a none-too-pleased Chris stepped in to stop her, not least because it would put man and wife in direct competition for listeners for early morning radio. 'He's turned into the most miserable man on radio,' jeered Evans. 'He's depressed because his wife was getting a job on a rival station. I don't see a problem. Chris is very good ... he's got no worries.'

The other Chris, Tarrant, usually managed to laugh off these attacks but this time round he'd had enough. He'd had to assure Ingrid there was no truth in the rumours about his relationship with Sophie, he'd had to endure the treachery of a former colleague, he'd been made to look a bit of a prat – and he rounded on Evans. 'Apparently Chris Evans – you remember him – thinks I'm very good on the radio, rather patronisingly,' he snapped. 'Chris, you're utterly pathetic and, if you weren't your own boss, you wouldn't have a job.' Associates of Evans responded by saying that Tarrant had lost his sense of humour. Bad feeling deepened all round.

Prince Edward and Sophie Rhys-Jones went on to get married and the whole affair, as far as the two of them were concerned, went away. But ironically, it continued to haunt Tarrant. A couple of months later he was asked just why he decided to yank up her T-shirt. 'It's not something I'm proud of,' said an unusually sombre Tarrant. 'I know I shouldn't have done it. There was nothing sexual about it. It was a pretty silly, thoughtless thing to have done and I'd rather it hadn't happened. It's not as though I make a habit of such behaviour. I mean, don't think I'm the type who goes around mooning.'

So it wasn't that he expected all the women he worked with to fawn on him? 'Nah, nah, nah,' protested Tarrant. 'The world just isn't like that. Eleven years ago I was just another jock, in fact the junior DJ, and we were all having a giggle. You'd be wrong if you thought Sophie was a young girl being forced to tolerate my stupid jokes.'

But it continued to rankle. In August 1999, three months after the snaps were published, Tarrant was still brooding. 'I feel sick to my stomach whenever I think about it,' he said. 'I always try and ignore stuff in the media but with the Kara situation I thought, I can't say nothing. The absolute garbage and snide insinuations written alongside the photograph were breathtaking. Sophie is, and was, a great laugh. She was always a totally moral, really decent girl. Of course I knew about the pictures – we all did. But they were no big deal and they weren't supposed to see the light of day. It was a huge betrayal of trust and the timing was just extraordinary – three weeks before Sophie was to marry.'

As for the other woman involved, Tarrant was scathing when asked if he and Kara could be reconciled. 'What would we have to chat about?' he asked. 'I have no idea what she is up to. I hear she's scared of coming back to the country. We haven't spoken and I can't imagine when we will. She made her decision and there is nothing I can do about that now.'

There were also questions about why Tarrant had ended up staying away from the wedding, even though he had been invited. Was it to spare Sophie's blushes? 'I was in Canada working. I was never going to the wedding,' he protested. 'From January I knew I would be out of the UK, full-stop. As it happens, it was just as well I wasn't around, because I would have been under focus again. That would have been the last thing they would have wanted on their big day. The reality was that we told Edward months before that I wouldn't be around.'

And there were continued ramifications for the *Sun* too. It lost the sponsorship of *Millionaire* – and all for the sake of a silly holiday snap.

11

A SADDER AND WISER TARRANT

Sophiegate might have been over, but its effects lingered on. Sophie herself, now the Countess of Wessex, had put recent events behind her, but the other two participants in the drama, Chris and Kara Noble, were finding it more difficult to move on. Tarrant, of course, still had his morning show and the hugely successful *Millionaire* to fall back on, but observers noted that for a time he was less at ease with himself than normal. 'I'm basically shafted by my own success,' he said. 'It's a good problem to have, but it's getting difficult.' It was a problem that the Tarrant of a decade earlier would have yearned for – but the Tarrant of today had been publicly made to look like a letch, and he wasn't happy. And he remained extremely bitter about you-know-who.

When one interviewer raised the subject of the photographs, Tarrant's reaction was theatrical. He publicly shouted for a plate of chocolate buttons. When they arrived he gobbled a couple and delivered a little homily. 'If Kara Noble came in here now, I wouldn't offer her one of these buttons,' he said. 'I'd say, "Why the fuck did you do it?" She has a history of disastrous affairs herself, perhaps that's why she did it. She will regret it. It was such a vicious thing to do. She is labelled the most hated person in Britain, a James Hewitt figure. She may be famous for what she did, but the stigma will last. She will find it difficult to get work in this country. I am a bad enemy.'

But, alongside the aggression, there was a certain amount of reflection. Tarrant's public persona was very much the lad about town who'd do anything for a laugh, but for the first time – and that includes the break-up of his first marriage – he'd been made to look really crass. He knew it too. 'It was a stupid, silly three seconds 11 years ago,' he said. 'I knew the pictures were about, but it was no big deal. My wife was disgusted with the pictures, but not with me – with Kara. And she had a long conversation with Sophie about it. There was no affair going on, that's all rubbish. Sophie was just a nice girl around the office. But we were both single and I wouldn't deny it if it was true.

'When I was first famous and women started throwing themselves at me, it was a constant pleasure, but I'm a faithful husband these days. I'm 52, for God's sake! It's hard to have a good, stable marriage, working long hours as I do, being away a lot, getting up before the kids, needing space for yourself and making time for the family. But I work at it pretty hard. It's all about compromise. I spend a lot of time with my family.'

Tarrant was also becoming increasingly sensitive to the charge that he had been unkind to Kara when they worked together. There had been a great deal of press speculation that Kara's actions were those of a woman scorned but, equally, some observers felt it was revenge at the way she'd been treated by Tarrant. If that was the case, her actions had backfired spectacularly – but, even so, Chris did not want to be seen as a woman-baiter.

'There are so many myths about this,' he said in response to a question about how the two worked together. 'People say she and I had this constant conflict between us, but I really got on very well with Kara. All this stuff about, "The things you said to Kara on radio were very unkind" – the things I say to Howard Hughes, my newsreader, are absolutely vicious and he's one of my best mates in the world! It's what we do for a living – and you actually can't do it to people you don't like. We got on very well with Kara for a very long time, but we felt quite disappointed that she left us just out of the blue.

'The thing is, the breakfast show has been number one in London for so long and the only period when it looked like we might in for a major head-to-head war was when Chris Evans first came on Radio 1 and Branson had just got Virgin FM in London. And that was the week Kara left us. The guys at Capital were saying, "Come on, Kara, you have got to give us a couple of months. Make the career move or whatever, but don't make it now – just wait for a little while."'

Once started, Tarrant warmed to his subject – and he was pulling no punches. It quickly became clear that he was still smarting not just from Kara's recent act of betrayal, but from her defection at a time when he might have needed her. For a man who put such emphasis on his working life, someone who let him down at a crucial moment was not to be lightly forgiven. Asked why she left, his answer was barbed in the extreme. 'I think she probably felt she was a good fun weather girl – and that was it. Capital repeatedly would not let her have her own show because they didn't think she was good enough.'

Chris then went on to tackle reports that her role on the breakfast show had been reduced. 'Her role was the same,' he said coolly. 'It was just unlikely to extend. She's not the world's greatest broadcaster. She had a great voice and a brain and she made people feel really quite horny about hearing the weather! But it was never going to be a two-handed show – there isn't room for it, not with me talking the amount I do! When she went to Heart, they gave her the breakfast show weather girl thing again – they wanted her voice in direct competition with us – and they wanted to give her her own show as part of the package. They tried the *Kara Show* – and basically, for whatever reason, it wasn't good enough, so she went back to doing the weather. At that stage you might get on to your agent and say, "Come on, what can we do?" You don't think, I've got that photo upstairs.'

Of course, Chris was not the only Tarrant who had to come to terms with what had happened. Ingrid had also been affected by the furore and she, too, was contemplative about her life with Chris. 'I think you get older and you get wiser,' she mused. 'When Chris and I first got together, I told him that I'd never tolerate him having an affair, but I've changed my view on that. Now, I don't think I would leave him and I know I'm almost giving him carte blanche by saying this. There is no question that it would destroy our relationship, but I would continue with the marriage because of the family.

'I've got four children – two from my first marriage and two, Samantha and Toby, with Chris – so I look at the family now. My two have already been through a divorce and they suffered in their own quiet ways. The two little children are so secure, so safe. They're one of the few children in their classes whose parents are not divorced. I couldn't ruin that for them. I would hate to see this house and family unit going. I just couldn't do that. It would kill every emotion I felt stone dead.

'I left my first husband because he had affairs, but now I think I copped out. It's braver to carry on with a marriage. It takes courage to put the children first. Staying in a loveless marriage is living half a life, but for somebody to do that for the sake of their children is admirable because they are making such a huge sacrifice. When my first marriage ended, the selfish side of me kicked in and I thought, I'm not going to have a half-life. I'm not going to compromise – not even for my children. Now I have more admiration for women who stick it out.'

Just as Chris had learned to compromise within the marriage, so had Ingrid. But Sophiegate, if anything, strengthened what was already a strong relationship. The couple had already weathered the stress that Tarrant's career put on the relationship and Ingrid worked, too, as a journalist and entrepreneur – she had a vintage Bentley she would hire out for weddings. A little fuss over an ancient photograph wasn't going to change that, and it was quite clear that Ingrid trusted her man.

'I don't actually believe Chris would ever have an affair,' she said. 'He isn't that clever. He is too straight. What you see is what you get. If he ever tried to be devious I would know. He couldn't cover his tracks. I've asked Chris if he's ever lied to me and he's sworn on Toby's life that he never has. I've never felt the need to ask if he had had an affair. I know he's in a profession where he's surrounded by people having affairs, but I honestly don't think he's got the energy and I don't think he'd risk everything we have together.'

Indeed, the marriage had clearly deepened over time. The two understood one another and supported one another. The initial attraction had turned into a very deep attachment. 'Over time, passionate love changes,' Ingrid said. 'We used to be rampant – at each other every second of the day, but as you get older, sex or lust is not the most important thing in a relationship. We're so worn out, we're not as active as we could be. So if you define being in love as the passion, the butterflies in the stomach, then no, I'm not *in* love, but I love him. It's calmer, less frenzied. Now we know each other so well and have this very deep love for each other. Chris is very tactile and is always giving me bear hugs. He's also a romantic. He writes me little notes when he goes away and I'll find one amongst my knickers saying "I love you" or under my pillow saying "Sleep well" or "I'll see you soon".

'It's the little things he does that have so much feeling. The other day I was writing an article for the magazine and he phoned me on his way home to check I was all right. I told him I was dying for a chocolate bar but couldn't be bothered to go out and buy one. When he came home, he walked into the study and said, Close your eyes and open your hands. He'd bought me a Caramel bar. It had been pouring with rain and he'd bothered to stop the car, go into a shop and buy me one.'

However, as both were quick to admit, the marriage was not always sweetness and light. Ingrid had, and has, a fiery temper and is quick to go off the deep end while Tarrant needs to go off on his own and fish. And then there was the minor matter of Ingrid applying for Kara Noble's job – a job that would have put her in direct competition with her husband. 'The only time there's ever been a real problem over my work was when I applied for Kara Noble's job at Heart FM after she was sacked for selling the topless pictures of Sophie Rhys-Jones with Chris,' she admitted. 'I think I did it because the Kara thing lingered. It was a terrible shock. People were saying, "Oh, poor you. How humiliating for you."

'But I didn't feel humiliated. I felt sorry for Sophie. Chris doesn't respect boobs. He's surrounded by them on beaches the whole time. It was just a silly thing that he did. That is exactly the way Chris is. He does silly things. I thought it was just playfulness, but the fuss wouldn't go away. The ripple effect of what Kara had done affected everybody. Suddenly I had this devil inside me and applied for her job. I thought, That's one in the eye for her. But Chris didn't want me to do it and it would have been wrong. It would have created problems. There would have been headlines like, "Ingrid in battle with her husband" or "Competitive couple".' And it was a battle Ingrid would almost certainly have lost.

And life did, finally, return to normal – whatever normal might be in Tarrant terms. As the fuss over Sophiegate finally died down, the fuss over *Millionaire* returned – with a vengeance. As Christmas approached at the end of what had been a truly tumultuous year, both personally and professionally, Tarrant was again dominating the television schedules, not least on the big day itself. In yet another unprecedented move, the decision was made to screen *Who Wants To Be A Millionaire* three times on Christmas Day: at 6pm, 8.30pm and 10.30pm. Just to make absolutely certain ITV won the ratings war, the first showing was to be followed by *Emmerdale* and *Coronation Street* and the second by *A Touch Of Frost*.

There was serious money at stake – and it wasn't the prize money on offer to the contestants. For the first 50 weeks of 1999, ITV's average peak-time share of the total audience figures was 38.9 per cent. But if, in the last two weeks of the year, ITV could nudge the average up to 39 per cent for the whole 52 weeks, it would trigger huge bonuses of up to £100,000 for top ITV executives, including ITV chief executive Richard Eyre and David Liddiment, who had given the green light to *Millionaire* in the first place. And what better way to push up that average than by swamping viewers with the nation's favourite game show?

'ITV didn't use to bother with the Christmas period,' said Steven Barnett, senior lecturer in communications at the University of Westminster. 'Little money came in because advertisers had spent it all in the pre-Christmas period. So ITV used to put out unexciting programmes and let the BBC have its one week's victory of the year. Yes, there's pride in not being beaten any more by the BBC and stopping all those negative headlines, but there's also those bonuses.'

There certainly were. On top of that, with the show yet to provide a £1 million winner, there was the added excitement that the win could happen on Christmas Day – which in turn led to concerns that Celador might try a little too hard in its quest to keep the ratings. The company, by now getting used to such accusations, was wearily dismissive. 'There's absolutely no question of our shows on Christmas Day being manipulated to get a millionaire winner,' said Andrew Wolf of Celador. 'Nor are we fussed at all by Chris Evans and his giveaways.'

And, indeed, ITV's strategy worked, with ITV beating BBC1 for the first time in 15 years in peak-time ratings. It pulled in 46 per cent of the evening audience, against BBC1's 39.7 per cent – although the Beeb did attract more viewers for the day as a whole. And it was not actually *Millionaire* that attracted the biggest viewing figures, but *Coronation Street*, as fans tuned in to see whether Martin Platt would have an affair with a fellow nurse (the answer was yes), followed by *The Vicar Of Dibley*, with *Millionaire* coming in third. The bonuses were duly triggered, the BBC condemned ITV for its overt commercialism and David Liddiment pronounced himself satisfied. 'The network has rounded off a fantastic year by giving our viewers a real treat with all their favourite shows,' he said.

By this time the show's popularity in the UK had been matched by its huge success in the US. And Chris could have experienced that success first hand. The ABC network had offered him a £5 million contract to present the Stateside show himself – but he turned it down, not least because he wasn't too keen on Americans. 'They keep insisting you have a nice day, but you know they couldn't give a toss what kind of day you have,' he said. 'In California, they've completely lost the plot.'

In any case, there was still a huge amount of excitement surrounding the show back home. Early in January 2000, garage owner David Neale won £250,000, only the second person to have done so – and then, just one day later, retired carpenter Peter Lee reached £500,000, a first for the programme. Unusually – and to push viewing figures yet higher – the show's bosses decided to reveal the win before it was screened. 'We wanted to make sure everyone knew about this in advance,' said a spokesman for the show. 'It's a great moment in telly history.'

But, needless to say, you couldn't please all of the people all of the time. While Celador bosses might have been forgiven for feeling vindicated by Lee's win, proving that the £1 million top prize really was on offer, a brand new problem leaped to the fore, with the show's bosses being accused of racism. The Commission for Racial Equality had been receiving complaints that there were very few black or Asian faces on the show and went public with its displeasure. 'What this situation means is that black or Asian people could be missing out on the chance of winning a million pounds,' said a CRE spokesman. 'We don't have a record of exactly how many complaints we have had, but there have been quite a lot – both on the phone and in writing. If your audience has an increasing number of black and Asian people, it makes sense to try and increase the diversity of the contestants.'

Adrian Woolfe of Celador responded by pointing out the very obvious fact that the show couldn't be guilty of racism, because only their voices could be heard when they applied to take part. 'The show is open to everyone who has a telephone,' he said. 'The only thing we know about any potential contestant is their name and phone number. The first time we see them face to face is when they arrive at the TV studio on the day of the show.' The CRE was not appeased, grumbling that, in that case, they should advertise the hotline number in the ethnic media.

Tarrant himself took the complaint seriously and said so. 'I would be delighted if a black contestant were to win a million,' he said. 'Anyone can come on the show. The last thing we want to do is to discriminate against anybody.' Matters were not helped when, in an investigation into how many members of ethnic communities appeared on game shows, *Millionaire* was amongst the worst offenders. 'We're mystified,' said Tarrant. 'People from ethnic backgrounds have as much chance of becoming millionaires on my show as anyone else. I want to say to those people, please ring us and have a go. There's nothing I find more abhorrent than racism.'

That was not the only problem the show was facing. For the first time since it began, *Millionaire* was not topping every rating going – the BBC's *EastEnders* had beaten it twice in a row, and one of the occasions featured the £500,000 win. To cap it all, Jacob's Crackers decided not to renew their sponsorship of the show, a decision seen in some quarters as a hint that the show might be losing popularity. Jacob's denied it. 'The deal was a wonderful promotion,' said Barbara Reid of Jacob's. 'Now we are going to redeploy our investment behind specific brands.'

Even Tarrant seemed to be voicing doubts about *Millionaire*'s future, saying, 'The programme is a phenomenon. It will be hard for me to decide when it has run its course.' Then again, he'd also been talking about giving up the Capital breakfast show pretty much from the day he started broadcasting, so it was difficult to know how seriously to take him. ITV certainly remained bullish. 'We are very proud of the show,' said a spokeswoman. 'There are lots of companies bidding to come on board.' In the end it was McDonalds who got the prize.

Doubts might have been surfacing in the UK, but elsewhere the programme was going from strength to strength. It became the first British quiz show ever to be bought up in Japan, while in the States, the quizmaster, Regis Philbin, was being awarded £13 million a year for his pains. In Russia, meanwhile, in one of the more bizarre programmes ever broadcast, four Russian presidential hopefuls took part in a one-off programme, with all winnings going to charity.

The foursome were Evgeny Savostianov, secretary-general of the Souz Truda Party, who came away with the highest winnings (32,000 roubles, approximately £1,000), Ella Pamfilova, chairman of the Healthy Russia Party, Stanislav Govoruklin of the People's Patriotic Party and Umar Dzhabrailove, an independent candidate from Chechnya. The quizmaster was Dimitry Debrov and all the programme lacked was Vladimir Putin, Russia's acting President and the one who went on to win the poll.

Back in the UK, Tarrant was up to his usual tricks. Having developed the habit of giving his Capital bosses sleepless nights as he publicly mused on whether it was time to quit, he now did just the same with the chiefs of Celador. He was nearing the end of his current deal in April 2000, and suddenly decided it might be time to step aside. 'Chris wants to bow out while the show is still a hit,' said a close friend (there were always plenty of close friends ready to talk whenever Tarrant was in salary negotiations).

'He knows it can only be fresh for so long and he wants to go before people start getting bored with him. Chris is a headstrong guy and he won't be pressured into doing something if he thinks there's a better option. He has an incredibly busy life.' There was speculation that Richard Madeley, Carol Vorderman, Des Lynam or even Dale Winton might step into his shoes.

Carol Vorderman did, in fact, take part in the show; she appeared in a charity edition alongside ITN newsreader Kirsty Young as part of ITV's Day of Promise appeal. The women won £125,000 and £64,000 respectively, while Carol commented, 'I haven't been so terrified since I did *Celebrity Stars In Their Eyes.*' 'They were both incredibly brave,' said Tarrant. Indeed, Carol later said that she had been so nervous that, 'I felt like kicking him in an awful lot of private places, frankly.'

Carol, in fact, was let down by the £250,000 question about Shakespeare (and she didn't distinguish herself afterwards, when she called the world's greatest ever playwright 'dull as dishwater'). What play, was she asked, featured the character Sir Toby Belch? It was, in fact, *Twelfth Night*, but Carol pulled out, having previously used her Phone A Friend to call her *Countdown* colleague Richard Whiteley. The £8,000 question had been: 'The Muslim era dates from the year in which Mohammed departed from which city?' Whiteley said he didn't know, but correctly guessed Medina. She also required the help of the audience when, for £16,000, she was asked, 'Who killed Billy the Kid?' It was Pat Garrett. Tiny Computers said they would match the sum Carol won and the eventual £250,000 went to the charity Express Link Up.

Kirsty, meanwhile, dropped out at the £125,000 question, which was, 'What was John Wayne's last film?' It

With good friend Sophie Rhys Jones at a charity event.

Chris's recent announcement that he is to leave Capital Radio's Breakfast Show will leave thousands of early-morning listeners bereft. He is pictured above with co-presenter Kara Noble.

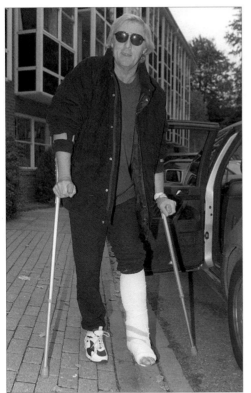
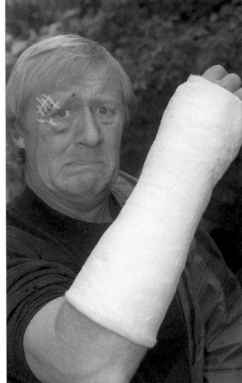

Top: Clumsy Chris sporting a broken leg and a broken arm – the result of falling out of a tree whilst fishing!

Bottom: Chris's boat, *Ben Gunn*, which was set on fire by arsonists.

Chris's biggest love is fishing. The picture (*bottom right*) was drawn by Chris and auctioned for charity.

Top and bottom left: Chris celebrates with Judith Keppel, the first person to win the elusive million on *Who Wants to be a Millionaire?*.

Bottom right: Whereas Judith Keppel used her brains to hit the jackpot, Charles Ingram – the Millionaire Major – tried to be a little sneakier. He is pictured here with his wife Diana.

Top: Chris at Elstree studios during filming for *Millionaire*.

Bottom left: Chris fools around with Peter Lee, winner of £500,000.

Bottom right: Chris puts his name to the *Millionaire* merchandise.

Chris is a man who works hard and plays hard. He is shown here pursuing three very different recreational pursuits!

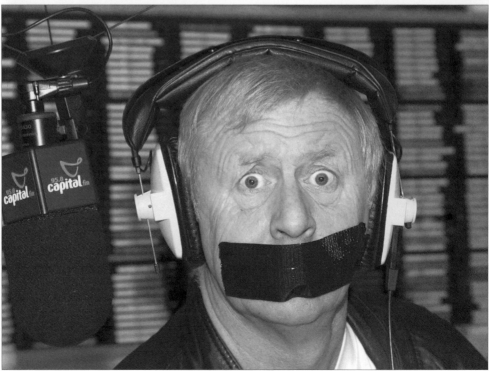

Top: The first time Chris has come face-to-face with his Madame Tussaud's model.

Bottom: The only way to keep motor-mouth Chris from talking!

was *The Shootist*, but Kirsty backed off and won £64,000. She used her lifeline to call, as a friend, BBC sports presenter John Inverdale when asked: 'Which sport traces its origins to a meeting at Huddersfield's George Hotel in 1895?' The answer, rugby league, earned her £64,000, which went to Centrepoint – and she wisely ignored the advice of the audience. Asked, 'The Gobi desert is on which continent?' the audience opted for Africa. Kirsty chose Asia – and pulled through.

Meanwhile, Tarrant appeared to have developed the Midas touch. Everything he was involved with turned to gold. In May 2000, Capital's half-year profits surged by £4 million to £22 million and a good deal of that was down to the breakfast show, which was pulling in yet more advertising. And, despite the doubters, *Millionaire* remained as popular as ever. Eidos, the games developer responsible for Lara Croft, announced plans for a computer game based on the television show.

'*Who Wants To Be A Millionaire* is a TV phenomenon and had captured the nation's imagination,' said Ian Livingstone, executive chairman of Eidos. 'Eidos will be aiming to replicate the appeal and success of the show with the ultimate challenge in interactive gaming.' And Tarrant himself would feature in the game, appearing in audio and video clips, posing questions and giving answers. 'Friends and families will now have the ability to play on their PCs and consoles,' said a cheery Chris.

Indeed, the game attempted to replicate the whole experience of the actual show as closely as possible. 'I recorded every possible permutation of every phrase I've ever said in the show,' Tarrant related. 'I put down all the variations of the spiel needed – "You've got £64,000, now £32,000 is safe and you've still got one life left" and so on. In all, it took about four hours to add my contribution.'

For his pains, Chris was awarded a 'small one-off recompense'. He also admitted that initially the programme really began on Capital. 'The show actually started here in the Capital Radio building, thanks to David Briggs,' he recalled. 'He was my producer and we used to do a game on air called *Double Or Quits*. Contestants starts with a pound, then got two for a correct answer and so on. I remember giving away £12,000 one morning and super-rich Capital was in an absolute flap over it, claiming we'd bring them to their knees. We countered that, actually, we thought they'd be all right, being the richest company in the northern hemisphere.'

But even Tarrant hadn't realised how successful the television version of the show would be. Briggs and co. had left Capital to work out the new format and ITV was not initially impressed when the idea was pitched. At first they heard nothing. 'They rang back about nine months later, out of the blue, and said they were very excited about the idea,' Tarrant recalled. '"We're going to call it *Cash Mountain*!" they said and when David told me the title I sighed. Next ITV came back again and said they would call it *Who Wants To Be A Millionaire?*. I sighed even deeper. My response was that it would never work. I could only think of the line from the song and it just sounded too cheesy. Of course, now I feel like the man at Decca who turned down The Beatles.'

As for the computer version of the game, Tarrant was not really considering playing himself. 'I have no idea with computer games, really,' he confessed. 'My kids are the computer game players. I just don't understand them, especially those with loads of explosions. For the past three or four years, my youngest son, who is now eight, has beaten me on everything I've ever tried, usually scoring 25,000 to 3!'

Across the pond, *Millionaire* was, if anything, even more successful than in Britain. 'We've made $220 million from *Millionaire* so far,' said an ecstatic Herb Granath, vice president of the ABC network. 'It's been absolutely fantastic for us.' Not only that, but it was even credited with saving the network. ABC had been struggling, but its ratings shot up with the arrival of *Millionaire*, with half the American population having seen at least one episode. There had also been a $1 million winner in the States – John Carpenter, after correctly identifying the US President who had appeared in the 1960s TV comedy *Laugh In* as Richard Nixon – although no one had yet got that prize in Britain.

However, managing to find the dark cloud that went with the silver lining, Tarrant promptly began expressing doubts about the future of game shows themselves. *Millionaire*'s popularity had been so great in the States that other game shows were suffering badly in the ratings, and Chris gloomily announced that the same fate could befall *Millionaire* itself. 'I don't know where programme makers can go from here and that is a serious problem,' he said.

'When you look at it, *Who Wants To Be A Millionaire?* is

killing off the other shows. When it comes to what the public would want from a new quiz, it's not just a case of upping the ante or even the money – it has to be about the tension of the game as well. Everyone is trying to find the answer to what the next quiz show will be, but as yet no one has come up with it and I don't see how they can. What broadcasters do now, I honestly don't know. I'm just lucky to be presenting the one that works.'

His gloom was shared by Monty Hall, who fronted the chart-topping *Let's Make A Deal* for 27 years. '*Who Wants To Be A Millionaire?* is killing it for other shows, because it has meant that the public are demanding much more from the genre than they ever have before,' he said. 'It soon won't be a prize of a million pounds – players and audiences will want to win five million. That could mean the entertainment aspect of the show going and the broadcasters having to fork out even more money.'

Poor Tarrant. Poor Monty. Poor ITV. To have such an amazingly successful show and only to be able to look on the dark side was, well, inevitable. For that's the problem in the insecure world of showbusiness: you're only as good as your last gig and, when you're at the very top, just where is there to go? And that was not the only problem bugging everyone involved – for as of yet, there had still not been one single winning millionaire.

12

THE TRIALS AND TRIBULATIONS OF TARRANT

Indeed, not everything was going entirely to plan. In June 2000, Tarrant's prized £140,000 boat was blown up. He had bought it at the Earls Court boat show six years earlier and, despite making jokes about what an expensive mistake it had been, had grown extremely attached to it. 'I got sozzled at the boat show and bought it for a disgraceful amount of money,' he confessed. 'When I woke the next morning, I thought I'd had a terrible dream. I had to go and look at my cheque stubs. And there it was. A figure followed by lots of noughts. I knew then I had either bought a boat or a Ferrari.'

And now it had been destroyed. Drunken yobs had been watching England crash out of Euro 2000 in a nearby pub. Looking for trouble they lurched out and climbed over a locked gate to reach the 40-foot *Ben Gunn*. After stealing Tarrant's fishing gear, the mob set fire to a leather jacket, which sparked a blast from a gas cylinder. The boat was totally destroyed.

Tarrant, understandably, was beside himself with rage. 'Whoever committed this outrage is completely stupid,' he fumed. 'My six children often spend the night on the boat. They could have been in danger. I'm disgusted by the hooliganism of this act. The people who did this have the same mentality as the football hooligans I witnessed on TV during Euro 2000.'

Chris shared the boat with his close friend Philip Davidson, who was equally devastated. 'We got a call from the neighbours around 12.30am,' said Philip's wife Debbie. 'When I looked out of the window, I could see a glow with the sky full of black smoke. By the time we realised the boat was on fire, it was impossible to save it. The tanks were full of petrol and it was a mass of flames.'

Indeed, her own four children also frequently slept on the boat. 'That's the most worrying thing,' Debbie continued. 'Anybody could have been on board. And it's close to a miracle no one was seriously injured. I feel so sorry for Chris. He was speechless when we phoned him with the news. My husband was so upset he couldn't even speak to him.'

Eventually it turned out that it had, in fact, been a deliberate attack – although not against Tarrant. Two men later admitted to arson, saying that Tarrant was not their target, but Philip Davidson. The duo had called on his son Stuart but, due to past disagreements, were asked to leave the house. They thus found the boat, splashed whisky around and set fire to it with a lighter. The two ended up sentenced to 21 months each in a young offenders' institution.

Tarrant was understandably fed up and did what he often did in these circumstances – he threatened to quit the show when his contract expired at the end of the next series, or at the very least cut down on his massive workload. 'I've been doing it for two years and I will have had enough by the end of next year,' he said. 'It has been an extraordinary success. It suddenly dawned on me that the thing I love and cherish most – my family – was being put at risk by my stupidity.

'So I now keep Saturday and Sunday very much as family time. I sometimes find myself thinking, God, my little boy is now eight. But I don't want to wake up one morning and think, Toby's ten and where have the last two years gone? No, no, that's all behind me at long last. I will be fronting the forthcoming series on ITV in September. But after that, I will have to think about the future. How long can I go on doing it? The trouble is, what will I do when I finish?'

And the BBC had finally had enough. Snide comments about the commercialisation of ITV and *Millionaire* were all very well, but the Corporation was getting utterly fed up of being regularly trounced in the ratings and decided to launch a counter attack. They would put on their own game show, complete with a presenter with a strong personality – and thus was born *The Weakest Link*.

Anne Robinson was to present the show, and while the top prize – £10,000 – was mere peanuts in comparison to its rival, this game was said to be all about the actual competition. '*The Weakest Link* is a competitive quiz show about skill, not money,' said a BBC spokesman. 'The modest prize – at its maximum limit – is equivalent to that of a family holiday or car. But the reality is that most contestants will win far less. The challenge will be in the testing of their skills in each elimination round.'

Celador could not have been less worried. While the show went on to capture the public's imagination, they still had *Millionaire* – and, of course, Tarrant. A new set of contract negotiations had recently taken place, during which he wearily decided he would stay with the show for a bit after all. In fact, according to the man himself, there was never any doubt that he would remain. 'It was utter bollocks,' he said of reports he was leaving. 'The ink was on the contract. It was signed and sealed.' And so Celador executives could sleep once more, content in the knowledge that they had their winning format and their winning presenter on side.

Tarrant's life was changing. He had been fairly famous for many years. Now he was really, seriously famous. 'There was a time two years ago,' he said, 'when I could walk the streets of London and people would not wind down their windows and say, "Eh, Chrissy, phone a friend, heh, heh,

heh." I don't know how many times a day that happens to me, but a lot. I always say, "Do you know, you're the first person that's ever said that to me," and they say, "Am I?"' Still, he wasn't complaining that much. Reports now put his personal wealth at about £30 million and, although he denied it, he was now clearly a very wealthy man. He was, however, keen to maintain the image of an ordinary bloke.

'Of course I get paid well,' he said. 'I work very hard. Whether I'm worth it or not, God knows. I mean, is a footballer worth £50,000 a week? That's the world we live in. I can't be bothered with showing off money. I've never been to Marbella in me bloody life. Or Barbados.'

And, despite his robust constitution, the work did take its toll. He found his own way of dealing with it. 'I catnap in the backs of cars,' he said. 'I remember doing an interview in Islington High Street and we had a 20-minute break, so I just stood against this wall and I was away with the pixies. This is how desperate my life had become. Somebody woke me up with, "Chris, can I have your autograph?"'

But he remained good at switching off. Tarrant had always taken exotic holidays, with and without his family, and it was the only way to deal with the circus his life had become. He even claimed work wasn't that important to him. 'I don't care very much about it,' he said. 'I am brilliant at switching off. I have been in Mexico for two weeks and I have to say that at no stage did I think about *Millionaire*, Capital Radio, *Tarrant On TV* or anything to do with how I earn my living.'

That business about earning a living was becoming an issue. Whenever he wanted to goad his rivals, cheer himself up or merely state the truth, Tarrant was fond of holding forth on the phenomena *Millionaire* had become. However, there was one small problem attached to that. While he kept talking constantly abut how ITV couldn't top its award-winning show, the same was true of its presenter. Where do you go when you've reached the top? 'A big problem I will eventually have to face is what I do after *Millionaire*,' he said. 'I cannot imagine going to another producer's office and talking about a new show and thinking, Will it ever compete with *Millionaire*? Because *Millionaire* has thrown every rule book out of the window.'

Tarrant and ITV weren't the only ones with the problem. Celador was also trying to match the success of its masterwork and finding it hard. In August 2000, they launched a new quiz, *The People Versus*, fronted by Kirsty Young. But it failed to ignite sparks and never took off the way *Millionaire* had done.

The eighth series was now approaching, with everyone concerned frantic to live up to the title of the show at long last. 'I can't wait – I'm desperate to make someone a millionaire,' said Tarrant. Of course, someone – or something – had already done just that. With *Millionaire* showing in 26 countries, and another 50 countries holding options to screen it, Celador was now worth a fortune – £300 million to be exact. The biggest winner was Paul Smith, whose 36 per cent stake in the firm was now worth

£118 million. And it was not just sales to other countries that made the money – the board game and book based on the quiz show were also coining it in.

In the States, the phenomenon that was *Millionaire* was equally strong, to the extent that it was even extending into the fashion world. This was due to Celador's insistence that absolutely everything in every country to which the format was sold must retain the exact details of the original version. 'It has to be copied exactly,' Tarrant explained. 'Celador is the production company which owns the rights and they say, rather bravely, if you want to buy this fabulously successful commodity, which will make you all very, very rich, then you must do it this way.

'They are very, very tough about it. They insist it is identical to our show – they even have to adopt my look, the dark suit and the tie. Oddly, in America, the suit is marketed as "The Regis Look" [after Regis Philbin, the US presenter]. Excuse me! I think they'll find it is actually "The Stephen-In-Covent-Garden Look" – he's the very nice man who works in the wardrobe department and decided what I should wear at the start.'

And now that Tarrant was so rich, why keep working? 'I'm just very lucky in that I thoroughly enjoy what I do for a living,' he said. And although he clearly enjoyed the money he was making – that soul searching that appeared every time a contract was up for renewal testified to that – many believed that was not the sole motivating factor in his continuing to work. 'He's not a money man,' asserted David

Briggs. 'Apart from his children and his family, I would say that his driving force is fishing.'

Not everyone was so generous. Some people said Tarrant was motivated by envy. 'It's because he hates to see anyone else doing well – especially Chris Evans,' said one former Capital colleague. 'He is a very jealous person and he has a massive chip on his shoulder.' Sally James, on the other hand, with whom Tarrant had kept in touch since the *Tiswas* days, revealed an altogether more caring side to the star. 'I'll always remember when my husband had a major operation about ten years ago,' she said. 'Chris said, "Call me the second you hear from the surgeon." It got to one o'clock in the morning and I knew he had the show the next day, but I called anyway. He picked up the phone and said, "I've been sitting up waiting for your call."'

Certainly, as far as his ITV bosses were concerned, Tarrant was a blessing. In the autumn of 2000, as the eighth series of the show began its run, ITV was as heavily reliant as ever on its jewel in the crown. It had been having trouble with the ratings, plunging to its lowest share of the TV audience in its 45-year history in early September, because of a combination of *Big Brother* on Channel 4 and dropping *News At Ten*. And it was determined to use *Millionaire* to get those ratings back up again. It had to to please the advertisers. 'ITV is to show the programme as much as it wants throughout autumn and winter,' said a source on the show. 'They need to shore up ratings and *Millionaire*, which regularly pulls in 12 million viewers, is there to provide them with a much needed security blanket. They are going to run it possibly every day and will make decisions about exactly which days on a weekly basis. If the viewers show signs of getting fed up they will have a break – before coming back again.' Even David Liddiment admitted all was not well, confessing, 'Our performance is not as good as I would have liked.'

But as soon as the show began its run, it became immediately apparent that all the drama and excitement generated by the previous series was still there. One contestant threatened to sue over the definition of vermicelli – he said little threads, the series said little worms – as he had been going for the £64,000 prize and ended up with just £1,000, while another declared that he would propose to his girlfriend if he won £16,000, and did just that.

It was, in fact, a very touching moment. Dave Bailey, a lorry driver from Laindon, Essex, had to answer nine questions correctly to get to his prize. Finally, on reaching the £16,000 question, he was asked: 'Which dish is named after a Napoleonic battle?' After correctly answering, 'Chicken Marengo', Dave punched his hand in the air to rapturous applause from the audience, as Tarrant told him, 'You're in trouble now, mate.'

But Dave didn't seem to think so. As soon as the show ended, he went backstage and proposed to his girlfriend Anne on bended knee. Much to the delight of all, Anne accepted, after which the couple told the producers that they had just bought a house together and needed £16,000 to pay for the wedding. 'It was fantastic, we've never had anything like it on *Millionaire* before,' said one delighted insider. 'The audience were on the edge of their seats. We did not know if he would actually go ahead and propose and were delighted when he did. It was a very emotional occasion. It's better than winning a million pounds – he's come away from the show with a wife.' Tarrant was equally pleased. 'It looks like we're going to have our first *Millionaire* wedding,' he said. 'I'd better go and buy a hat.'

And Tarrant, as ever, was having to manage his own domestic life. It was back to the 18-hour days again, but as he approached the show's 100th edition, he was keen to stress that his family remained supremely important to him. 'I know that I spend most of my time at work, but I've always said you can never be too busy for sex,' he asserted. 'It is the perfect way to unwind and such an important part of a relationship. Work is not as important as having a happy family. Ingrid and our six children mean the world to me and I spend as much time as I can with them. My first marriage failed because I was a workaholic and I'm determined not to make the same mistake again. But it is difficult with the 18-hour days.

'I'm knackered at the moment. The other night I finished filming at 10.15pm. I had a drink with a contestant who'd won a quarter of a million pounds and my car arrived at 11pm. I arrived home about midnight, but I didn't go to bed until about 1am as I needed to unwind, and I was up four hours later to do the breakfast show. That is why I'd rather have a cosy night in with Ingrid than go to a party with the cast of *Big Brother*. That isn't my idea of a fun night out. I make as much time for Ingrid as I physically can. I love being with her, we have a great life, love one another and will be together until the day we die.'

Indeed, Chris was keen to put the 'four women in a day' image firmly behind him. All was now domestic bliss. 'Ingrid and I have a great sex life,' he continued. 'But, if I've got any regret, it's not having slept with Tina Turner. She has the most attractive legs. Ingrid has legs like that – they're a lot whiter, though. She understands me and we have built up an amazing level of trust over the years. She's my rock and organises all my domestic stuff.'

Tarrant also emphasised the importance of his children in his life, explaining that, because of his work schedule, he could sometimes go for days without seeing them. 'It is hard but, if I thought my kids were genuinely deprived of love, I'd rearrange my life,' he said. 'I pick them up after school when I'm not working. I'm often the only dad in the playground among all the mums. A couple of months ago we went to Mexico, then flew to New York and came home on the *QE2*. I completely switched off from work. It was absolute bliss.

'I earn decent money, but never spoil my kids. My eldest daughter is at school with a girl who was given a new Mercedes worth £90,000. It's pathetic. I said I'd go halves when my daughter buys her first car – as long as it's not a Mercedes. I want my kids to grow up well-rounded individuals, not spoiled brats.'

It was a punishing regime and one that would have taken its toll on a much younger man, but somehow Tarrant managed to keep going. And his stamina was all the more surprising, given that he didn't follow a fitness regime. But he had been very sensible in one way. Despite the long hours, the stress and the pressure, Tarrant was very firm on the subject of drugs and why not to take them. 'The only thing I've ever taken is paracetamol,' he said firmly.

'I wouldn't know where to buy drugs or how to take them. I won't even touch sleeping pills because it frightens me that something the size of a pinhead could knock me out for eight hours solid. One of my mates took half a tablet of LSD and then climbed on to the roof of a Holiday Inn. He thought he was Batman and was waving his arms about, ready to take off. But luckily we caught him in time. That experience frightened me to death and I vowed never to touch drugs afterwards.'

But he was still more than capable of knocking back the hard stuff. Onlookers were amazed to see him going on a bender with some colleagues from Capital Radio: starting at lunchtime in the Soho restaurant Zilli Fish, Tarrant downed a bottle of tequila over the course of the day – and at 3am the following morning he was the only one left standing. Clearly, despite the lack of both exercise and sleep, Tarrant's was a constitution that could withstand almost anything.

It wasn't only ITV who was bothering about schedules and that was to result in one of the biggest TV clashes of them all by the end of the year. Even when it was first announced, it made headlines. The BBC had recently moved its main newscast from 9pm to 10pm, and were thus pushing other programmes around. The decision about what to pit against *Millionaire* was a difficult one – and the Beeb eventually decided to go for *One Foot In The Grave*. Such was the popularity of the latter, featuring Victor Meldrew, that BBC bosses thought they might even be able to conquer the all-powerful *Millionaire* in the ratings battle – not least because they had a very strong storyline later in the year.

It was a big gamble, especially as there was no sign at all that the public was tiring of *Millionaire* – quite the opposite, in fact. At the National Television Awards in October, on the night of his 54th birthday, Tarrant was given the Outstanding Achievement Award – by this time, well deserved. *Who Wants To Be A Millionaire?* also did well, winning Most Popular Quiz, an award voted on by the public. To mark the occasion, Tarrant's father Basil was summoned on to the stage dressed as the Phantom Flan Flinger from *Tiswas*, bearing a flan that was actually a birthday cake. Tarrant said he was stunned and honoured to receive the award, before apologising to Ingrid and the children for never being at home. 'Turn your TV on and you'll know where your dad is,' he went on.

That pretty much applied to everyone else in the country too. *Millionaire* continued to excite, not least when it featured its biggest gambler ever. Duncan Bickley had reached the £500,000 question when he was asked: 'What was the name of Amy Johnson's plane in which she flew to Australia?' Saying, 'It's only money,' Duncan used his 50:50 lifeline and then chose *Pegasus*, rather than the correct answer, *Jason*. His winnings dropped back to £32,000 and, although he appeared to take the news relatively calmly, the audience gasped with horror.

Afterwards, Duncan, 39, from Brentwood, Essex, remained relaxed. 'I'm totally happy,' he said. 'I always said I wanted to win £1 million, not £250,000. My decision to gamble was made on the basis of what I would be able to handle better afterwards: being wrong and losing £218,000 or being right and not having gone for it and living with the fact that I hadn't seized the day.' It also made for gripping television.

Meanwhile, the Irish series of the show had just begun, fronted by the veteran presenter Gay Byrne, who came out of retirement to do so. It seized the public imagination immediately, with over 100,000 callers trying to get on in the first two weeks alone. The palaver was just what you would expect. The question writers were told to keep their identities a secret for their own sakes, while massive security surrounded the computers generating the questions. 'Every one of the question setters will put their questions and answers on a computer specially formatted so that, even if someone gets their hands on a disc, they cannot open it,' said a thoroughly overexcited insider. 'The questions are then put on to another disc, which is collected by a secret team of couriers. The security is unbelievable. It is at a high level because it has to be.' Indeed, the hope in Ireland was that a millionaire would be created there before it happened in the UK.

The BBC, never very happy when *Millionaire* was hogging all our screens, had now found something else to moan about. Just as the Beeb launched the new *Ten O'Clock News*, ITV decided to ditch an ad break at the end of *Millionaire*, which meant it ran into BBC news airtime by four minutes. It's 'dirty tricks' snapped BBC insiders, although ITV was able to retaliate when it pointed out that the Beeb had started *One Foot In The Grave* three minutes earlier than *Millionaire*. Both sides were taking no hostages in the ratings war – and were determined to win.

And, of course, *Millionaire* continued to generate human drama. Jean Thompson, 43, won £8,000 on the show, just a couple of weeks after her former husband appeared in court for bigamy. After marrying her and giving her a son, Christopher, he ran off to the French Foreign Legion, after which it emerged he'd been married before and not divorced and had then married a third wife. 'It's a wonderful windfall that will make a huge difference,' she said. 'When he walked out on us, Christopher and I were left with nothing. I'd been supporting him and spending all my money on him. He gave nothing back in return. I've struggled ever since and battled to get myself back on track. Suddenly life is a whole lot better for Christopher and me. I'd hoped to come away with a little bit more, but £8,000 will do very nicely.'

Much to ITV's chagrin, Victor Meldrew and co. were the

initial winners in the ratings war, bringing in 10.2 million viewers to ITV's 4 million. ITV affected not to worry, claiming that overall that evening, they had won. 'ITV remains Britain's favourite channel, even though the BBC threw in everything they had, including their strongest programmes. It was the one night they thought they would win. They must be disappointed.' The BBC, meanwhile, was making plans to screen an hour-long *EastEnders* special, as well as showing *The Weakest Link* in the evening. The stakes were getting increasingly high.

And with no millionaire winner on the horizon, Celador were having to come up with other ways to keep the viewers transfixed. One bright idea was to stage a Mr and Mrs version of *Millionaire* to be shown over Christmas. It was actually taken from the Greek version of the show, where it had proved hugely popular. 'Just imagine the arguments!' said a gleeful Tarrant. 'I thought watching the two of them together would be great – the friction would be fantastic! What often happens here is that the man is sent on the show because he's the breadwinner. But sometimes he's as thick as two short planks and it's the wife in the audience who is miles brighter.' And, of course, two brains were better than one. And that elusive millionaire had still not been found ...

Despite all his success, however, Tarrant still kept returning to the subject of Chris Evans. Evans by now was a very rich man, having bought his own radio station, Virgin, where he was still working as the breakfast show presenter. 'He's clearly done something right,' sniffed

Tarrant. '[But] I don't think you can make radio work when everyone around you is on your payroll. I have never understood the sense of that. I don't have people here who say, "Chris, that was fabulous." They say, "God, you sounded shite this morning."

'Professionally it is so dangerous. I would not like to come off at 10am and go straight into meetings with the sponsors, the accountants, the managing director, the money men. I can't tell Chris how to do his job and handle his life – he has clearly made a lot of money somehow. But it certainly appears from the numbers that some of his talent has got lost. I don't think he has turned in anything good for years. Maybe he thinks he doesn't need to any more.' And Tarrant had a point. On the one hand, of course, there was a good degree of professional rivalry between the two men. But on the other, Tarrant had by now outlasted pretty much all of his rivals, staying at the top of both television and radio. Capital knew it too and awarded him £1.1 million in share options as a one-off grant equal to his salary, all designed to keep him at the station.

Back at *Millionaire*, yet more human drama exploded on to the screen when a long-lost father and son were reunited after 23 years. Mark Durnall, 38, was watching the programme one night when 'Tony Durnall from Wolverhampton' came on the show. 'That's him!' yelled Mark, at which his wife Victoria made contact with the programme and organised a reunion. The two had been living just six miles apart, after Tony lost touch with his son after splitting from his mother. Mark had even put ads in the local papers trying to track him down.

It was an emotional moment. 'They can keep the million now I've found my son again,' said Tony, 64, who never actually made it to the hotseat. 'What the show has given me is priceless.' Victoria was responsible for the reunion, arranging a meal in secret for the two to meet up. 'I got Mark to the hotel saying I'd booked a meal and his face was a picture when he saw his dad there,' she said. 'It was a marvellous moment and we were all in tears.'

In November, Kate Heusser became the first woman and only the second person to win £500,000 on the show. 'I was so nervous towards the end, I had to tuck my hands between my legs to stop them flying around,' said the 44-year-old ex-solicitor. 'I don't think it will change what we as a family do with our lives, but it will make it easier.' The family planned to move to a new and bigger house, while Kate concentrated on her new career as a writer. She also planned to buy a dog for one son, Gregory, sailing lessons for the second, Edward, and a trip to a Grand Prix race for her husband Peter, a kitchen designer.

Tarrant was delighted. 'Kate was absolutely brilliant,' he said. 'We were all so delighted for her. She was very brave and very cool under pressure. I think I was more scared than she was. I was really holding my breath, thinking, This is it, this is going to be the big one. She was a truly great contestant.'

It was a timely win in many respects. The size of it reminded viewers that the £1 million prize was really on offer and, on top of that, there had been some criticism of the show for not featuring enough women. Now here was a woman who was only the second person to have got to half a million pounds. And another woman was about to feature pretty prominently on the show too. For now, at last, two years after the programme began, someone was finally about to become a millionaire.

13

WHO WANTS TO BE A MILLIONAIRE?

It was a conspiracy! cried the nay sayers, for which read the BBC. They did it deliberately to steal our thunder! It was a set-up! It wasn't fair! We wuz robbed!

The cause of the upset was this: *Who Wants To Be A Millionaire?* had, at long last, produced a millionaire winner. But the winner wasn't just any old contestant: it was a member of the aristocracy and, even more than that, a distant cousin of Camilla Parker Bowles. The two women even looked a bit similar. And, even more to the point as far as the Beeb was concerned, the big win, the first ever in the UK to get the jackpot, went out on the very same night as the final episode of *One Foot In The Grave*, the episode in which Victor Meldrew took his final bow. The BBC had been hyping it for weeks, and so for the big win to come through on exactly that night seemed more than just a coincidence.

As accusations flew, the winner herself seemed bemused at the furore her win had provoked. Judith Keppel, 58, a garden designer from Fulham, west London was an unlikely figure to have provoked such a row. A grandmother who is closely related to the earls of Albemarle, she won the £1 million prize after correctly identifying Henry II as the husband of Eleanor of Aquitaine – and after waiting three minutes to discover if she'd picked the right answer. 'I was a nervous wreck,' she confessed. 'It was the longest three minutes of my life.' As the audience burst into uproar, her tearful daughter Rosie ran on to the stage to get to her mother. 'You're in a worse state than Mum!' said a clearly delighted Tarrant. 'It was so exciting,' he continued after the show. 'The atmosphere in the studio was incredibly intense. Judith was a fantastic contestant and I was delighted to hand over the cheque.'

And she really was a real aristocrat: she was educated at St Mary's, Wantage, Oxfordshire where she left with eight O levels and two A levels and was remembered by her contemporary, Liberal Democrat MEP Emma Nicholson as 'good fun and a nice person'. One particularly close friend was Candida Lycett Green, the late Poet Laureate John Betjeman's daughter and later, coincidentally, a confidante of Camilla Parker Bowles.

In 1959, at the age of 17, Judith came out as a debutante at a dance in Londonderry House at the foot of Park Lane hosted by her cousin, Lady Mairi Bury. Lady Mairi herself is the aunt of the Marquess of Londonderry and his two sisters, one of whom is Lady Annabel Goldsmith, widow of Sir James Goldsmith.

Judith's father was Lt-Commander the Hon Walter Keppel, second son of the ninth Earl of Albemarle. She is also the great-great-niece of Alice Keppel who was the mistress of the Prince of Wales, who later became King Edward II, after they met in 1898. Alice's great-granddaughter is none other than Camilla Parker Bowles. Alice herself was married to George Keppel when she fell in love with Bertie, as the King was formerly known, when he was 56 and she was 29. She had two daughters, the second of whom, Sonia, was Camilla's grandmother.

The news of Judith's aristocratic heritage made almost as much of a plash as did the win itself. 'How absolutely extraordinary that a close relative to an earl should be on a programme like that,' said the late Peter Townsend, the social consultant for *Tatler* magazine. 'Who says the aristocracy of today is effete? They're clearly alive and kicking.'

And Judith was not at all badly off even before her win. Twice divorced, she lived in a three-storey house in Fulham, near Bishop's Park. Her first husband was Desmond Corcoran, co-owner of the Lefevre Gallery in Mayfair, which sold the works of LS Lowry. The couple had three children, Rosie, an artist, Alexander, an art dealer, and Sybilla, before divorcing in 1980. In 1985 she remarried, to Neil Shand, a comedy writer to, amongst others, Spike Milligan and Jasper Carrott. Carrott is a shareholder in Celador, which just enraged the conspiracy theorists still further, convinced as they were that the win had been more than simply by chance. She and Shand later divorced.

Judith reacted quite calmly to her win, celebrating with just a soft drink after the show. She had used lifelines: asking the audience when questioned about Tony Blair's home country for £16,000 – Scotland – and phoning a friend for a question about Shakespeare. 'It's wonderful,' she said. 'It's a huge sum of money. Money has not been a terrible problem and I'm obviously not on the breadline. But I'm really looking forward to spending it. I felt overwhelmed when I won the million-pound question. It was like being in a football match – there was an incredible roar from the audience. It was so exciting.'

The BBC was beside itself as *Millionaire* overshadowed Victor Meldrew's final exit, with 13.9 viewers against the BBC's 10.7 million. Rumours were rife that the questions had been made deliberately easier, or that Judith, through her second husband, had some idea of what lay ahead. 'The last time there was a big winner was November 2, when it coincided with an hour-long episode of *EastEnders* on BBC1,' it snapped. 'It seems too much of a coincidence for it to happen twice.'

Richard Wilson, the actor who played Victor Meldrew, was equally angry. 'I think it was planned,' he said. 'There's no doubt about that. It is ever so slightly suspicious that ITV had a millionaire winner the night of Victor's death. It seems a bit unfair to take the audience away from Victor's last moments on earth.' He really took it to heart, as his agent

Sarah MacCormick later revealed. 'Richard is most upset by what has happened,' she said. 'He feels that, after playing Victor for so long, this has been a very sad anticlimax for the poor old chap.' Nor did his co-star Angus Deayton help when he admitted he was one of the many who missed the final episode, given that he was watching *Millionaire*. 'I have to admit that I missed the show,' he said brightly. 'I was recording for the BBC and when I went into the hospitality room everyone was watching the end of *Millionaire*. So I must admit I watched that.'

Celador was blithely unconcerned, describing the allegations as 'preposterous'. 'We've waited two years for someone to win £1 million,' protested a spokesman. 'Why should we have waited so long if we could rig the show? The BBC really is scraping the barrel.' Tarrant, meanwhile, was as weary as ever. 'The questions are hard,' he said. 'We refused to dumb the questions down. We always said it would happen one night. We always said it would come out of the blue and it has.'

David Liddiment was actually quite angry at the accusations from the BBC. 'That the BBC should stoop so low as to suggest there was tampering going on maligns both the production company which makes the series and the ITV network,' he snapped. 'It saddens me that the BBC is conducting itself in this underhand manner. It's childish. Instead, it should be joining ITV in celebrating the fact that five million additional viewers tuned in to terrestrial television on Monday night. The programmes that achieved this were a fantastic comedy and a terrific quiz.' The BBC was not even remotely mollified and demanded a recount. (In fact, later in the year this blew up in the Corporation's face, and it was forced to issue a lengthy apology for suggesting anything was amiss. But at the time, feelings were running high.

Judith remained unruffled. At a press conference the following day, she announced, 'I felt very calm. It's nice to be rich.' Tarrant pranced around to lighten the proceedings for the cameras, at one point pressing pursed lips against Judith's cheek, but she was unmoved. 'Look like you've won £1 million,' begged one photographer. 'This is what it looks like,' said an unsmiling Miss Keppel. She was going to pay off her mortgage, she said, perhaps move to a grander house and make a contribution to a tiger charity run by her daughter Rosie.

All that aristocratic stiff upper lip was clearly coming into play, but she did relax a little when she described how she went about getting on the show. Although not a gambler herself, 'It is very exciting and I like the psychology behind it,' she said. She added that she thought she could win at least £1,000, which would cover the cost of the phone calls for getting on the show, an assumption which was more than fulfilled. Indeed, she phoned so often to make sure she would get her place, calling the hotline 75 times, that BT sent her a warning note telling her her bill had soared. 'I think they believed I had a teenager who was suddenly phoning peak-rate lines,' she said.

And she had even been thinking of moving to a cheaper

place. 'In fact, recently I found living in London far too expensive and wanted to move to the south-west of France where life would be cheaper,' she said. 'I phoned the show because I have wanted to compete for about two years and it was worth the investment.' None other than Camilla Parker Bowles had her say, commenting, 'Of course I'm thrilled for her.'

And the actual filming had been full of tension. After getting to the £16,000 win with the help of the audience, Judith then had to wait 24 hours for the next recording of the show. The next crisis arose when asked where the town of Duffel, of coat fame, lies. She didn't know and went 50:50, after which she correctly chose Belgium as the name sounded French. 'I did not want to waste the Phone A Friend lifeline, because I knew my friends wouldn't know the answer,' she said. 'I said to myself, "To hell with it, I'm going to go for it."'

At £125,000 she phoned her long-standing friend Gilly Greenwood when asked to complete this stage direction in Shakespeare's *The Winter's Tale*: 'Exit, pursued by a bear.' Gilly was a wise choice. She had been the editor of the *Literary Review*, before becoming deputy controller of arts at LWT. She had also read the play for A level. 'I knew the answer straight away,' she said. 'Even if you haven't read that play, "Exit, pursued by a bear" is a famous stage direction.' As for Judith's winnings, the pair had made no agreement to share.

'I agreed because I thought it would be fun and I am quite good on arts and literature,' said a modest Gilly. 'I certainly didn't expect anything. I am sure she will buy me dinner. Perhaps we will go somewhere more upmarket than last time. It was scary waiting for the phone to ring. I was starting to relax, thinking Judith didn't need me – then Chris Tarrant came on the line.'

When it finally came to the big one, Judith relied on her own knowledge. 'I was fairly sure,' said Judith. 'I did A-level history.' And had she ever met her famous cousin? 'I don't really know Camilla that well, but I did meet her a few times when I was a child,' Judith recalled. 'Apparently her great-great-grandfather was the brother of my great-grandfather.'

There was much talk of how wealthy Judith really was. On the one hand there were the class warriors claiming that a rich woman didn't need even more money, while on the other friends were saying that just because she had a 'posh voice' didn't mean she didn't need the money. One woman whose daughter had attended the same school as Rosie, the £13,440-a-year St Mary's Catholic School in Ascot, Berkshire, recalled the glory days when Judith was still married to her first husband.

'There were a lot of wealthy girls at the school, but Rosie's family was easily one of the richest,' she said. 'The first time I was invited home to tea I couldn't believe it. It was a massive Georgian house set in acres of grounds. There was an army of uniformed staff including housemaids and butlers. It was like staying with the Royal Family. She [Judith] was like Penelope Keith in *To The Manor Born*, but not so snobby. We would spend days lazing round the pool having fabulous food delivered to us by servants. The family also had a villa on a Greek island. I was amazed when Judith first appeared on *Millionaire* on Saturday. She always struck me as bright and gutsy. I said to friends on Saturday that, if anyone could do it, she could.'

She had also been left some money by her father, who had died 14 years earlier: a third share of a £700,000 estate. 'She can't help the fact that she's not a school dinner lady, single mum, living on income support,' said an indignant (and much richer) Tarrant. On top of that, she was believed to have owned four paintings by well-known artists: the first a portrait of Charles II's illegitimate son the Duke of Richmond, painted by John Wootten. There was also a portrait of the Marquis of Tavistock by Francis Cotes, as well as paintings by Thomas Hudson and Henry Weigall. But life had not always been smooth – Judith ended up attending Alcoholics Anonymous – hence the soft drink after her win – and, as her brother Colin, a Stuttgart-based architect, once said, she'd had 'an up-and-down life'.

Rather surprisingly, Judith took to her new celebrity like a natural. She did interviews and went on a tour of the nation's television studios, where she got the chance to put her side of the story. 'It annoys me that people assume I'm extremely rich because of my connections,' she said. 'It seems you're either living on the breadline or you're filthy rich. The truth is that I'm neither. I'm not struggling, but I don't have pots of money. None of my close family is rich and this money is going to make a huge difference to us.' She signed up with a newspaper to write a weekly quiz and started giving advice on garden design. She then even used her newfound celebrity to suggest that hard-up toffs use the show as a way of restoring their fortunes.

'I think toffs ought to line up in rows and sign on and fight back a bit,' she announced. 'What they don't seem to realise,' she continued, 'is that you can have toff relations, but equally you can have not very much money. My particular bit of the family are not rich. My grandfather sold our family house in Norfolk after the war because they thought that way of life was over. It's the last throw, really. They are stamping on us now. There's no power base, no House of Lords.'

As calls to the barricades go, this was an unusual one, but no matter. Celador was happy. It had received so much negative publicity through never having produced an outright winner that the mutterings over Judith's win were as nothing. In fact, the company positively relished the publicity and, from then on, it was back to business as normal. And the show kept providing satisfying human drama stories, as well as big wins. Chris Elliott, a teaching assistant on £10,000 a year and the next contestant after Judith, borrowed £100 from his mother to help pay the fares from Castlefield, West Yorkshire for him and his girlfriend Sally Booth. He promptly won £125,000.

'The TV company paid for flights to London, but I didn't have the £50 to cover taxi and train fares to get us to Leeds Bradford Airport,' he explained. 'Luckily Mum gave it to us and a bit extra to spend on food and things. I'll be able to pay her back now and buy her a nice treat.' He said he would use the money to pay off his debts, set aside some money for his two-year-old daughter Katrina and buy a new car. 'This money is a Godsend,' he declared. 'Chris Tarrant knew how much this money meant to me. He was over the moon when I won.'

That, of course, was another secret of the show's success – Tarrant's special empathy with the contestants. It was quite true: he wanted them to win and another £125,000 winner, Ben Whitehead, testified to that. 'It was totally unreal, I was completely spaced out by it all,' the BA student from Liverpool Hope University confessed. 'I was so drunk when I rang up to get on the show that, when they called me back, I couldn't remember the questions I'd answered correctly.

'Then, when I won the fastest-finger round and ended up in the hotseat, it was really freaky. It got more and more unreal as I answered each question correctly. When I got to £8,000, there was a commercial break and, as the cameras went off, Chris leaned over to me and said, "Don't you dare f***ing lose it!" I don't swear much, so it took me by surprise and really woke me up to what was going on.' Shortly afterwards the second ever £500,000 winner – a tipster for the *Racing Post* called John Randall – correctly identified a spelunker as being someone who explored caves.

It was at this point that Tarrant's other career – breakfast show DJ – suddenly featured again, this time in a scenario not much to his liking. In an extraordinary note to investors, bankers UBS Warburg sent Capital's shares plunging when analyst Simon Mays-Smith said that Chris should leave the programme. Capital's audience figures were being squeezed, he said, by rival stations appealing to a younger audience and Tarrant would not be able to appeal to the same people himself. Of course, he totally missed the point: that Tarrant's appeal is more successful than his rivals precisely because it is wider. Capital rather wisely ignored the notice, having already proven they were willing to pay through the nose to keep Chris on.

Nor was Mays-Smith Tarrant's only critic. In an odd outburst, the then Education Secretary David Blunkett had a go at the show. 'In the 80s, yuppyism was seen as the end of civilisation,' he said. 'We are back to *Who Wants To Be A Millionaire?* now. The people who produce these programmes have a pretty low view of the rest of the world, except when it comes to their own families.' Celador dismissed the comment as a politician merely trying to grab headlines.

Millionaire ended the year on yet another high: it had become the most popular television show on the planet. It was now showing in 80 different countries, including Russia, of course, where it was called *O Schastlivchik!* which means Oh Lucky Person! This was not necessarily the case – in Russia the Phone A Friend often gives the wrong answer deliberately. Apparently the Indians face the hardest questions, the Germans are the most serious about it and the Japanese have it the easiest. And in India, more than money was on offer: one prize was an evening out with the Bollywood film star Amitabh Bachchan. In Turkey, the show was watched more than regional belly-dancing competitions – and back in Britain, the contestants' weakest subject area was politics.

Tarrant himself was now gaining recognition from all quarters. He was a subject on *This Is Your Life* and made it into that catalogue of the rich and famous, *Who's Who*, in which he listed his hobbies as fishing and croquet. A model of him appeared in Madame Tussaud's. He became the most watched figure on British television, with an 'exposure factor' twice that of the runners-up, Richard and Judy, while his name appeared in the *Collins Concise English Dictionary*. The *Millionaire* board game was doing just as well as the show itself: it sold almost double the quantity of its closest rival, Nintendo's Pokemon Yellow, in the last quarter of 2000.

A third contestant bagged the £500,000 prize – Steve Devlin, from Belfast. He provided the prerequisite drama that seemed to accompany so many of the big wins: he had actually been on the show before, but had walked out when his nerves got the better of him. This time, of course, he walked away a wealthy man.

And it really was all the emotion going on behind the scenes that made the show such compulsive viewing, as Tarrant himself recognised. 'Greed is just a handy label,' he said. 'There's a lot of money around, so people think it must be about greed. Money is not irrelevant, but the millionaire tag is not that important. It's a soap, a drama. It's real people.' He was right. Their backgrounds continued to play a part in the proceedings, such as the occasion when student David Stainer was abruptly dismissed from *The Weakest Link* – and then went on to Tarrant's show to win £64,000.

In April, the show managed to produce a second millionaire

– 54-year-old science teacher David Edwards, who correctly answered 'trees' to the question: 'If you planted seeds of Quercus Rober, what would you grow?' It was actually just the latest in a series of prizes for David, who also won *Mastermind* in 1990 as well as being Mensa's 1985 Super Brain Of Britain. 'I knew it was a type of oak,' he later confided modestly, 'because the word 'cork' comes from the Latin *quercus*.' He then returned to his job as physics master at Denstone College, Staffordshire.

Could it get any better? Yup. Celador Productions, apart from raking it in, were given the coveted Queen's Award for Enterprise for selling the show all over the world. 'In half of the countries of the world, you can ask someone, "Do you want to phone a friend?" and they'll know what you mean,' said chairman Paul Smith.

And then Tarrant landed the accolade to end all accolades: he was invited on to *Desert Island Discs* – and you know you've made it when you've got Sue Lawley quizzing you about your life. Tarrant mused about his future, as usual, saying there was another year in it for him, but after that, who knows? He discussed the idea of making documentaries – 'There are loads of offers on the table,' he said. 'You never know.' He hoped a woman would take over fronting *Millionaire* he said, but, 'Please don't let Anne Robinson do it. She's far too kind and cuddly.'

As for the success of *Millionaire*, he added, 'People initially thought I was being cruel and we do tease them. But what you get is this extraordinary cross-section of humanity. It works because it's incredibly simple. I've had a very lucky life. I really enjoy my life. I pass people at bus stops who are clearly not getting much pleasure in their lives.'

Tarrant's choices, for the record, were as follows:

1) Cavatina from the *Deer Hunter*
2) A Day in the Life – The Beatles
3) Nights in White Satin – The Moody Blues
4) The Bucket of Water Song
5) Tequila Sunrise – The Eagles
6) Tears in Heaven – Eric Clapton
7) Another Day in Paradise – Phil Collins
8) Angels – Robbie Williams

His book would be *Silence of the Lambs* by Thomas Harris and his luxury, touchingly, his lucky sixpence.

Even so, for the first time ever in his 25-year career, Tarrant's lifestyle finally caught up with him and he had to take a day off sick from food poisoning. 'Myself and a few friends were in France yesterday and we ate some French muck which really disagreed with me,' the patient reported from his sickbed. 'I'm really knocked out. I've had a very punishing work schedule recently. With my breakfast show on Capital I have to wake up at five every morning. And with *Millionaire*, I don't get home till midnight. I've usually got the constitution of an ox and I have done the shows back to back for so long, but I suppose my defences are a little low. Come hell or high water, I'll be back in tomorrow. I'll pop a couple of pills to sort my stomach out – that should do it.'

He made a speedy recovery and was soon up and about, indulging in one of his favourite pastimes – having a go at Chris Evans. Evans had just had a spectacular fall-out with his bosses at Virgin Radio – he'd sold the station by now and married the much younger Billie Piper – and Tarrant was merciless in taunting his rival. Talking before he hosted the Commercial Radio Awards ceremony in London, he mused, 'I think he will take some time out and sort out his marriage. I hope he hasn't got a serious drink problem, I don't think we are talking about clinics and George Best land. But I think everything that's happened to him recently has been too much for him. Having £60 million in the bank is hard to handle and he clearly hasn't handled it very well.'

As *The Weakest Link* grew in popularity – there was even talk of putting it up against *Millionaire* – Anne Robinson also became a target. No one could do malice in a caring way the way that Chris could – and indeed, he let rip. 'There is room for all sorts, I just wouldn't want to do that,' he began. 'It is strangely insidious, sitting there with all the answers, pretending to be very clever. I don't think it is a great show. I suspect the bubble will burst. The people who are on it are cannon fodder for the Robinson ego.'

As Evans took off on a year-long break with Billie, Tarrant did what he always does – he went back to work. In August 2001, he hosted another celebrity version of the show, with winnings going to charity: this time, it featured *Coronation Street* stars. David Neilson, who played Roy

Cropper, was the most successful, winning £64,000, which he donated to Mencap.

Tarrant seized the opportunity to talk about quitting the show. 'I plan to slow down a bit and maybe take six months out to go travelling,' he mused. 'I'm always taking week-long breaks when I go to places like Canada, Africa or the States, but I've never been to India or China. You can't do China in a week and I'd like to see it properly while I'm still fit enough to enjoy it.'

In September there was just a ripple of the first and, to date, only scandal to rock the show. A Major Charles Ingram scooped the £1 million prize, only the third person to do so, but something seemed amiss. Someone appeared to be coughing too much in the background. The cheque was suspended and the police were called in.

And now millionaires appeared to be rolling in thick and fast. Just as no one was able to climb Mount Everest until Sir Edmund Hillary managed it, after which it practically became a tourist trail, so Judith's £1 million win seemed to pave the way for a whole crowd of winners. And, like Ms Keppel, this one wasn't exactly scraping the barrel either. Robert Brydges, a 47-year-old retired banker, correctly answered the question: 'Which scientific unit is named after an Italian nobleman?' He used his 50:50 lifeline and answered, 'Volt', having recognised the name from the poem *Horatio On The Bridge*, which he'd read to his children. 'I wasn't in much doubt and was using the 50:50 because I would have looked like a prat if I had got it wrong and not used it.'

It immediately emerged that, actually, Robert was already a millionaire. He had retired 18 months earlier and now owned a £1.5 million townhouse in London's Holland Park, as well as renting a rural retreat near Romsey, in Hampshire. Answering the charge that, since he already had a lot of cash in the bank, he shouldn't have entered the quiz, he replied, 'I wouldn't go along with the argument that the competition shouldn't be open to anybody. The whole point of it is that it's random. You could be a peer of the realm or unemployed and get on. It's a level playing field.' And, aside from providing for his family and his children's education, Robert's first requirement was a modest one – a washing machine.

The rivalry between Tarrant and Anne Robinson was on show for all the world to see in October's National TV Awards. *The Weakest Link* was becoming ever more popular and it was thought that it might even topple *Millionaire* for the prize of most popular quiz show – but it didn't. Tarrant won for the third year in a row, although he didn't get most popular entertainer – an award which went jointly to Ant and Dec.

Tarrant and Robinson finally went head to head when their programmes were scheduled opposite one another, with Chris winning hands down. He got 10.2 million viewers, 43 per cent of the audience share, against Robinson's 3.8 million. Tarrant was jubilant. 'Anne is ridiculously harsh to people who are going through the hoop anyway,' he said.

'It just seems unfair. I know it's television and not to be taken too seriously, but I can't stand to watch her take the mickey out of people because of their ignorance. I don't think *The Weakest Link* is a very good game – it doesn't work – and Anne's strange way of presenting I find very bizarre. I don't like the way she dismisses her contestants and, because she has the answers there in front of her, she comes across so patronising.'

Millionaire was now crossing yet more boundaries. It was to feature in a special edition of *Only Fools And Horses*, the first ever such collaboration between the BBC and ITV, with Del on as a contestant, before ITV put a spanner in the works in an argument over repeat fees. It also featured in the film *About A Boy*, starring Hugh Grant and Rachel Weisz.

Meanwhile, Tarrant showed himself to be a thoroughly good sport when he took part in a day-long sponsored silence on air to raise money for the homeless charity Centrepoint. *Dead Ringers* mimic Jon Culshaw pretended to be Tarrant, as he stood in for him on air, kicking off by introducing Aqua's single 'Barbie Girl' – which Chris loathed – as his favourite song. Indeed, he took quite a ribbing as friends and family called in threatening to reveal his secrets. Ingrid also called to say she'd put £52,000 on his credit card. His studio mates joined in the fun. Engineer James opened the door to ask, 'Do you want that tenner back I owe you?' Tarrant nodded furiously. 'I'll take that as a no then,' said James.

A fishmonger friend rang in to say that Tarrant often called in at his shop to buy something when he'd failed to make a catch. A barmaid called Cathy at Soho's Lamb and Flag looked at his written plea for a pint after the show and then announced, 'I can't read. What are you going to do about that, then?' Tarrant banged his head on the bar. But he managed to stay quiet, raising £10,000 in the process. 'I never, ever want to do it again,' he said afterwards. 'I'm very good at talking. I've made a whole career out of it. Even when they nail the coffin lid down, I'll still be talking. Keeping quiet for 24 hours is the hardest thing I've ever done in my life.'

The year ended on a high, with Tarrant broadcasting from Capital on Christmas Day. But he was to face a tumultuous 2002. For someone had tried that little bit too hard to become a millionaire.

14

THE MAN WHO WANTED TO BE A MILLIONAIRE – TOO MUCH

The early reports were vague. Someone had been coughing too much or too little or at odd times – no one was really sure. What the programme makers were sure of, though, was that something distinctly odd had gone on on September 10, 2001, the night that Major Charles Ingram, who served with the Royal Engineers, had appeared on *Who Wants To Be A Millionaire?* – so odd, in fact, that they called in Scotland Yard. 'We can confirm that the Metropolitan Police Service are investigating an allegation regarding a television programme,' said a spokesman for the Metropolitan Police. ITV, meanwhile, withheld the £1 million prize money. No one really knew what was going on.

It very soon emerged that the Ingram family was no stranger to *Who Wants To Be A Millionaire?*: Ingram's wife,

Diana, a 35-year-old nursery nurse, had already appeared on the programme and won £32,000, as indeed had her brother, Adrian Pollock. And Ingram's own conduct as a player had been strange, given how much he ended up winning. He had already used up two lifelines – Phone A Friend and Ask The Audience – by the time he'd reached the £4,000 question, and these were the easier ones. The final, million-pound question was: 'What is the name of a number that is followed by a hundred zeroes?' The major answered, 'Googol' – correctly.

And then there was the matter of that coughing. Someone in the audience had certainly got a frog in his throat, and one that appeared to have a certain consistency. When a question came up to which the right answer was A, there would be one cough, B would merit two coughs and so on. If that were not all funny enough, Ingram kept rehearsing the questions and the answers – out loud. 'He kept changing his mind and going through all the answers,' said Andrew Silke, who was in the audience. 'He said he wanted to equal the £32,000 his wife got.'

And of all people to attempt such a scam, this particular couple seemed such a surprise. They had met as students in London and spent their marriage moving from one army house to another, while the major had had a six-month stint in Bosnia. Now with three daughters, Portia, Rosie and Hester, they were living in Easterton, Wiltshire, while Ingram, who trained at Sandhurst, worked on a nearby army base. And they appeared bewildered by the fuss. 'I wish I knew what was going on,' said Major Ingram. 'I have no idea why they are investigating me. I don't know what there is to investigate.'

As matters began to get more serious, Ingram issued a statement through his solicitor. 'He is stunned, bewildered and devastated at the action that has been taken and feels that the effects leave his career in the Army and livelihood in tatters,' it read. 'Mr Ingram has stated he will do all in his power to fully protect his legal position and restore his reputation. Mr Ingram is known to be of impeccable character.' Indeed, they went on, Ingram was prepared to start legal proceedings against Celador if they didn't get a move on and pay up, adding, he 'strenuously denied that he was part of any irregularity in any stage before or during the course of his entry in to the competition'. Ingram's wife, Diana, tried to put a brave face on it. 'Our family has had quite a bit of luck on this show,' she said. 'We all love it. We will continue to watch it every time it's on because we enjoy it so much.'

Celador remained firm. 'ITV and Celador Productions confirm that the Metropolitan Police are investigating apparent irregularities relating to an episode of *Who Wants To Be A Millionaire?*,' it said in a statement. 'Until these investigations are concluded, ITV has postponed transmission of parts of the episode in question. No further comment will be made at this time.'

Soon the mystery cougher came to light. Tecwen Whittock, a 51-year-old lecturer from Whitchurch, Cardiff, admitted to coughing, but denied there was anything odd about it. 'It was cold in the studio and a lot of people were coughing,' the head of business studies at Pontypridd College in south Wales protested. 'I can't believe he was helped in such a way. Yes, I did cough while the major was in the hotseat – but many others did too.

'There were 200 people in the studio. I certainly wasn't trying to help him. I sat with nine other contestants, waiting for our chance to be in the hotseat. It wasn't in any of our interests to help him – we wanted him out so we could have our go.' Indeed, Tecwen had even been the next contestant on after the major and, after fluffing the £8,000 question, left with just £1,000. 'I cocked it up and now I wish somebody was there to cough for me!' he said.

It was not a wise joke to make in the circumstances. The police were taking the allegations of impropriety seriously and called in a voice expert to analyse the mysterious coughing. In addition to that, a three-man inquiry team was checking out the backgrounds of the 200-strong audience, to see if there were any associates of Ingram present, as well as analysing his phone records. 'The police have indicated that this might be a drawn-out affair,' said a spokesman for Celador. Ingram, meanwhile, was stepping up on the defensive, accusing Celador that 'mud sticks'.

In November, the police made three arrests on suspicion of trying to defraud the programme's producers: Charles and Diana Ingram and Tecwen Whittock. Celador, meanwhile, had introduced stringent security measures, including body searching everyone who came on the show to prevent cheating. Mobile phones were banned from the studio and infra-red lights were installed. Someone was also hired to watch the contestant's behaviour to spot anything funny going on. 'We have to treat everyone who walks into the studio as if they were criminal masterminds,' said a sombre Paul Smith. 'Of course, they are not, but it's sad that's the approach we have to take.' It was also, sadly, inevitable. One million pounds is an awful lot of money and, with hindsight, someone, somewhere, was almost bound to have a go at breaking the rules.

It was not until the following August that the Ingrams, alongside Tecwen Whittock, finally appeared in court, charged with 'conspiracy to procure the execution of a valuable security by deception' and 'procuring the execution of a valuable security by deception'. And it was not until March 2003 that the three finally had their day in court, with Nicholas Hilliard prosecuting. In his opening address, he told the court that Major Ingram kept repeating the questions over and again, while Whittock kept repeatedly coughing.

However, once Whittock himself was in the hotseat, the cough disappeared. 'You may think it inevitable, human nature being what it is, that where £1 million is regularly on offer, someone somewhere will have thought how it might be possible to improve their chances in getting their hands on the money by cheating,' Hilliard intoned. 'That is exactly what the prosecution say happened in this case.'

Ingram's first-day appearance was without incident. It was then that he got to the £4,000 question, before filming halted overnight. 'It was the next day, when he returned, that the coughing began,' said Hilliard, before playing the jury the tape of 15 questions. By the end, the coughing was clearly audible. Ingram's 'frequent changes of mind', he continued, 'coincided with the coughs'.

As the trial unfolded, the public was also as gripped by the proceedings as they were by the programme itself. One detail after another was gobbled up: the Ingrams, it emerged, did not go to the bar with everyone else after the win – rather, they went to their dressing room where they had a blazing row. Ingram could quite clearly be heard telling his wife to 'shut up', hardly the happy behaviour of a newly rich couple. Then it came out that Ingram had a mock-up 'Fastest Finger' keypad at home on which he practised – not suspicious in itself, but clearly the behaviour of someone determined to win.

And so the replay of the show began as follows.

Question 1 for £100: On which of these do you air laundry? A. Clothes dog. B. Clothes horse. C. Clothes rabbit. D. Clothes pig. Ingram answered B.

Question 2 for £200: What name is given to a person who is against increasing the powers of the European Union? A. Eurosceptic. B. Eurostar. C. Eurotrash. D. Eurovision. Ingram immediately answered A.

Question 3 for £300: What is butterscotch? A. Shortbread. B.

Pavement game. C. Flower. D. Brittle toffee. Ingram answered D.

Question 4 for £500: Which of these is the nickname of a famous Scottish army regiment? A. Black cat. B. Black Widow. C. Black Sea. D. Black watch. Ingram answered D.

Question 5 for £1,000: The Normans, who invaded England in 1066, spoke which language? A. German. B. Norwegian. C. French. D. Danish. Ingram said that it was a bit tricky as the Normans originally came from Denmark, but eventually said, 'I'll go with French.'

Question 6 for £2,000: In *Coronation Street*, who is Audrey's daughter? A. Janice. B. Gail. C. Linda. D. Sally. Ingram said he'd never watched the soap and had no idea. He asked the audience, who chose B.

Question 7 for £4,000: The River Foyle is in which part of the United Kingdom? A. England. B. Scotland. C. Northern Ireland. D. Wales. Ingram thought it was Scotland, but phoned his friend Gerald from south Wales, who directed him to C.

The recording for the first day ended there. The next day, Major Ingram was cheery, telling Tarrant, 'I've got a strategy.' And so questions began again.

Question 8 for £8,000: Who was the second husband of Jacqueline Kennedy? A. Adnan Khashoggi. B. Ronald Reagan. C. Aristotle Onassis. D. Rupert Murdoch. Ingram went through the options. 'I would have thought it was Aristotle Onassis,' he said. There is a loud cough. 'I'm pretty confident it's Aristotle Onassis.' Another loud cough. 'You only live once,' said the major and chose C.

Question 9 for £16,000: Emmenthal is a cheese from which country? A. France. B. Italy. C. Netherlands. D. Switzerland. Ingram answered D with no coughing. 'I'm counter attacking,' he said.

Question 10 for £32,000: Who had a hit UK album with *Born To Do It* in 2000? A. Coldplay. B. Toploader. C. A1. D. Craig David. There is no coughing and Ingram says he doesn't know any of the artists. He seems to go for A1, then chooses Craig David. After a commercial break – 'Bastard, bastard, bastard!' he shouts at Tarrant to audience laughter – he finds out he is right.

Question 11 for £64,000: Gentlemen versus Players was an annual match between amateurs and professionals of which sport? A. Lawn tennis. B. Rugby union. C. Polo. D. Cricket. Ingram says he thinks cricket is the right answer and there are two coughs. Twice more he repeated cricket, twice more there are coughs. It is correct. 'You're shaking, Major,' said a cheery Tarrant, handing him a cheque for £64,000.

Question 12 for £125,000: *The Ambassadors* in the National Gallery is a painting by which artist? A. Van Eyck. B. Holbein. C. Michelangelo. D. Rembrandt. 'I think it was either Holbein or Rembrandt, I have seen it,' said the major. Loud cough. 'I'm sure it was Holbein.' Very loud cough. 'I'm sure it was Holbein, I'm sure of it, I think I'm going to go for it.' Cough. 'Yeah, Holbein.' It was, of course, right and as Tarrant handed over the cheque he enthused, 'You're fantastic, just fantastic. You're getting better as we go on.'

Question 13 for £250,000: What type of garment is an Anthony Eden? A. Overcoat. B. Hat. C. Shoe. D. Tie. Ingram paused. 'I think it's a hat,' he said. Cough. There is some deliberation, in which he says he's sure it's a hat, provoking another cough. It is a hat and he goes through.

Question 14 for £500,000: Baron Haussmann is best known for his planning of which city? A. Rome. B. Paris. C. Berlin. D. Athens. 'I think it's Berlin,' said Ingram. 'I think, I think it's Berlin. Haussmann is more a German name than an Italian name, a Parisian name or an Athens name. If I was at home, I'd be saying Berlin.' A loud cough follows, and then some spluttering, in which the word 'No' can clearly be heard. Ingram pauses. 'I have to rethink, I don't think it's Paris,' he says. Two coughs. He mentions Athens and Rome and then says, 'I would have thought it's Berlin, but there's a chance it's Paris. Yeah, I think it's Paris.' Loud cough. 'Yeah, I'm going to play,' said Ingram. 'Wait a minute, where are we?' says Tarrant and repeated the question in full. 'It's either Berlin or Paris, I think it's Paris.' Cough. 'I'm going to play Paris.' 'You thought it was Berlin, Berlin, Berlin, you changed your mind to Paris – it's brought you £500,000,' said Tarrant, hugging him. 'What a man, what a man – unbelievable.'

Question 15 for £1 million: A number one followed by 100 zeroes is known by what name? A. Googol. B. Megatron. C. Gigabit. D. Nanomole. 'I'm not sure,' mused Ingram. 'Charles, you haven't been sure since question two,' Tarrant replied. Ingram repeated all four answers. 'I think it's a nanomole but it could be a gigabit,' he said. 'I'm not sure, I don't think I can do this one. I don't think it's a megatron and, I have to say, I don't think I've heard of a googol.' Loud cough. 'Googol, by a process of elimination, I actually think it's a googol, but I don't know what that is. I don't actually know what a googol is but it's the only chance I will ever have of winning £1 million.' 'It's the only chance you'll ever have of losing £468,000 – can I put that into the equation?' said Tarrant. 'You are going for googol just because you've never heard of it.' Ingram ran through the answers again, with another cough after the word googol. 'I'm going to play,' he said, to gasps from the audience. Tarrant tells him he doesn't have to, but Ingram repeated that he would go for googol. Another cough. 'Please don't go for a break,' said Ingram – but his plea was unheeded, at which point a floor manager came down to tell the audience not to talk about the question: 'There is a serious amount of money at stake.' The cameras started up again, at which point Tarrant fluffed his line and had to be filmed again. There was yet another break, filming started up – and finally Ingram learned he had won £1 million. As he punched the air, close to tears, Diana ran down to hug him as Tarrant crowed, 'You are the most amazing contestant we have ever, ever had. I am so glad to have met you. I'm proud to have met this guy, he's an amazing human being.'

With hindsight, of course, something was clearly wrong, but that is a condensed version of something that in reality took hours to film. Ingram took up to 15 minutes to answer the questions and, in the fevered atmosphere of the studio, excitement was at such a pitch that the odd cough went relatively unnoticed. It was only afterwards, when editing the tapes, that the film crew began to realise what had happened. And looking back at Tarrant's reaction, it is also evident that it wasn't only Celador that Ingram was cheating, but also Tarrant's own good nature.

As the trial went on, it was clear that major planning had gone into the scam. Ingram tested using four vibrating pagers dotted around his body, but abandoned the idea, something that was discovered when the police went through his phone bills. Eve Winstanley, a researcher on the show, told how the couple both appeared tense and upset after filming had ended and turned on her after she was sent to his dressing room to help everyone lighten up. 'He raised his arms up in the air and said, "Don't start, I have got things to do, you don't understand,"' she said. 'Then he told me to "get out".'

If Ingram had been trying to make himself appear guilty, he couldn't have done a better job. To make matters worse, Diana's brother Marcus Powell was present during filming and asked to be seated in the VIP area, rather than with the audience, where he was seen repeatedly using his mobile phone. Other audience members were also beginning to have their suspicions about what had really gone on.

Graham Whitehurst, another hotseat contender, could clearly see Whittock from where he was sitting. 'It became evident fairly early on that Mr Whittock was coughing – he was coughing rather ostentatiously right the way throughout the show,' he said. 'It was pretty irritating, because he didn't seem to be doing much to stifle it.' Indeed, Whittock was even given a glass of water to help. It didn't work, and Whitehurst finally became suspicious during the £500,000 question. 'During the course of that question, I became absolutely certain that they were colluding with each other by Tecwen Whittock coughing in the right place,' he said. The last question totally convinced him.

'My hobby is pub quizzes and that question had been asked a couple of times – I knew before it came up,' he said. 'Before then I had been fairly sure that Tecwen Whittock and the major were in cahoots on the previous question. I was leaning forward, glaring at Tecwen Whittock, thinking, Don't you dare, don't you dare, that's how I was feeling. I was listening out for googol, waiting to see what he was going to do. I was absolutely certain he was going to signal. As he had done with the other questions, Major Ingram seemed to dismiss googol initially. He went all the way around the houses as he had done throughout the show and, as soon as he got to googol, Tecwen Whittock went, "cough cough". I am 100 per cent sure because I was studying him. I was focusing on Tecwen Whittock to see what he would do at that point as soon as the world googol was mentioned.' When he won, Whitehurst was unable to join in the fun. 'I thought, What's going on here? Have I just witnessed what I've just witnessed? Or is my mind playing tricks on me? It seemed like I was involved in some weird experience. It was amazing. I didn't applaud and I didn't cheer.'

Tarrant himself took the stand and told of his astonishment when he first realised the major might have been cheating. 'Certainly, I couldn't believe it,' he said. 'You don't expect anyone to come on a show like that to cheat.' He said the major's behaviour was 'extraordinary and very hard to fathom', but that he'd heard no coughing himself. 'Not specifically, because there is just so much going on at the time – wild applause, the major himself, extraordinary behaviour, excited behaviour and very-hard-to-fathom behaviour. I am so focused, particularly at that level because you are talking about £1 million, unless there was somebody in the audience with Morse code,' he said.

As Tarrant's testimony went on, he revealed some of the secrets of the show's success. He himself didn't have access to the answers, so that he couldn't inadvertently give any hints by his facial expression: he drew laughter in the court by demonstrating his 'strange' expression when the questions were being answered, saying, 'It goes like this.' He got another laugh when asked if he'd hugged Ingram: 'Yes, but in a manly way,' he said. And it was he himself who chose when to go for a break: 'It's quite fun to make them sweat a bit,' he admitted. Nor did the couple seem tense to him. 'They seemed as normal as people who have just won £1 million would in that situation,' he said, but added that 'I had been told there had been quite an unpleasant exchange.'

When Ingram himself spoke, he told the police that he'd decided to act as if he was on a military mission. 'I decided I would have to do everything I could to get to £1 million,' he said in an interview read out in court. 'That meant taking calculated risks, weighing up the answers and taking account of the risks just as I've had to do in the Army. You never have enough resources in the Army. You decide to limit the risks to achieve the mission. That is exactly what I did that night. I had seen other people on the TV not go as far as they could have done. I decided I would take limited risks and go for it, that is what I did. The money was secondary to trying to answer the question. I looked at each of the answers, tried as best I could to delete answers that were too ridiculous and weigh up the options on the remaining answers and, if I felt 80 per cent confident or more on a particular answer, I would go for it.'

Tecwen Whittock – who also denied having an affair with Diana – was equally robust in his defence. 'I don't need to cheat to get the money,' he declared. 'Why would I put myself in serious risk of a prison sentence when I have never done it before? I would not do it. It would be against my morals. I am a family man.' Ingram denied even knowing Whittock – although it did emerge that Diana had made a string of calls to him before they all went on the show.

Ingram himself was nearly in tears when he took the stand, saying that his life had been ruined by what had happened. 'I'm not on medication now, but for about a year I was,' he said. 'It was awful. Living with this great cloud over you is dreadful. It's been extremely difficult to live with. Not wishing to exaggerate it, we have had the cat shot at and people driving past shouting "cheat" if we are eating in the garden. I have had my car vandalised and so on and so forth. It's been absolutely dreadful.'

Summing up what he called 'a most unusual case', Judge Geoffrey Rivlin, QC, said that either Ingram got all the answers right by himself or he was helped by an accomplice who coughed at the right moments. The jury withdrew and asked to see three tapes again. Eventually all three were found guilty, with the Ingrams being fined £50,000 and given an 18-month suspended sentence and Whittock fined £17,500 with a 12-month suspended sentence. The judge told them he was not jailing them as, 'You've been shamed in the most public way and your reputations ruined. Having regard to your positions in life, that must in itself be a severe punishment indeed.' Nor did he want to deprive the Ingrams' three children of their parents.

But it was a strange case. Indeed, he said, 'I am not at all sure it was sheer greed that motivated this offence. I'm sure that all three of you were besotted with quiz programmes and ambitious to be successful on a major TV show. It was this that caused you to beat and – it has to be said, cheat – the system.'

Celador made the best of a bad business and made a documentary about the affair. Tarrant himself was clearly disgusted by it all. 'I feel very sad about this whole business, but I cannot really feel any sympathy for the perpetrators,' he said. 'This was a very cynical plan, motivated by sheer greed. It is hugely insulting to the hundreds and hundreds of other contestants who have come on the show, just hoping for much smaller amounts of money, but prepared to try and win their money honestly. Since we started in 1998, we have given away over £35 million to the most incredibly varied and very brave cross-section of people. For a large percentage of them, the money they have won has changed their lives for the better. It is unthinkable that anybody should come on the show and think they could go home with the biggest prize of all dishonestly. Of course, I spotted nothing at the time – he was the most extraordinary contestant, constantly changing his mind from one possible answer to another, and behaving in the most erratic and hard-to-follow fashion. I think we all now know why.'

In the aftermath of the trial, new facts emerged about the defendants. Tecwen Whittock, a father of four, had appeared on a string of game shows himself, including *Sale Of The*

Century, but had never done very well. By 2001, he had debts of £37,341 and was desperate to appear in *Millionaire* to pay off what he owed. But, given his past record of non-achievement, he decided he needed someone's help and decided on Major Ingram's brother-in-law, Adrian Pollock, who had just won £32,000 on the show, where he was accompanied by the other brother, Marcus Powell. He tracked Pollock down to his home in the Vale of Glamorgan and the two of them went for a drink. They hit it off.

Meanwhile, Diana also got on the show, where she won £32,000, £14,000 of which she loaned to Adrian, who was having some financial difficulties. On Pollock's advice, eventually, Whittock began to ring Diana as well as Adrian to talk about what to do if he got on the show. At around the same time, Diana and Charles, who themselves had loans and credit card bills amounting to about £50,000, were beginning to hatch their plans regarding *Millionaire*, and finally recruited Whittock to join them.

After the show itself, some Celador staff were already so suspicious that they frisked the couple before they left the show. Paul Smith was in Wembley, seeing to another show, when Celador's lawyers rang him and asked him to come and view the tapes. He was up until 3am watching them, by which time he was convinced something was really wrong.

Meanwhile Graham Whitehurst had suspicions of his own. Unaware that the producers had already called in the police, he rang a number of broadsheet newspapers, as well as the BBC and ITN, to tell them he thought the pair were in cahoots, but as this coincided with the terrible terrorist attacks on September 11, no one was really interested. He did, however, get a bit of tabloid interest, and also contacted the Met anonymously.

Tecwen Whittock resigned from his job and did some after-dinner speaking. The Ingrams have always maintained their innocence and continue to aroused a good deal of interest. It is possible their story will be made into a film. And Celador got excellent ratings for its documentary into the affair. *Who Wants To Be A Millionaire?* continues.

In 2003 it was announced that, after all the speculation, Chris was finally leaving Capital Radio, to be replaced by Johnny Vaughan. 'I'm now off to enjoy life without the early starts and I won't miss the alarm going off every morning,' he told his fans. And after 17 years in the hot seat, who can blame him? But if one thing is for sure, one door closing will undoubtedly lead to another opening for Britain's best-loved personality, and whatever the future holds for Chris, it is bound to be bright...